Sounds and Signs

Sounds and Signs

Aspects of Musical Notation

by

HUGO COLE

London

OXFORD UNIVERSITY PRESS

New York · Toronto

1974

Oxford University Press, Ely House, London W.1

GLASGOW NEW YORK TORONTO MELBOURNE WELLINGTON
CAPE TOWN SALISBURY IBADAN NAIROBI DAR ES SALAAM LUSAKA
ADDIS ABABA BOMBAY CALCUTTA MADRAS KARACHI LAHORE
DACCA KUALA LUMPUR SINGAPORE HONG KONG TOKYO

ISBN 0 19 317105 8

Printed in Great Britain
by Fletcher & Son Ltd, Norwich

Contents

Preface   *page* 1

PART ONE   The Background

    1   Origins and uses of musical notation   6
    2   Communication in general   10
    3   Communication in music   16
    4   Response: how to read music   22
    5   The psychology of notation   28
    6   Failures of communication   32

PART TWO   The System at Work

    7   Lines of approach   36
    8   Pitch   44
    9   Time   57
   10   Dynamics and timbre   74
   11   Articulation and phrasing   82
   12   Mood, sense, and silence   90
   13   Auxiliary notations   95
   14   Specialist notations   105
    a)   Ethnomusicologists' notations   105
    b)   Notation of electronic music   112

PART THREE   Today and Tomorrow

   15   Literary attitudes   122
   16   Towards a determinate notation   127
   17   Experiment and reform   131
   18   Where now?   149

List of Sources   154
For Further Reading   157
Index   158

We are grateful to the following publishers for permission to reproduce short extracts from music which is their copyright, as follows:

Boosey & Hawkes Music Publishers Ltd. (Bartók: *Mikrokosmos 113, 133, 140, 143,* and *146;* Britten: *Turn of the Screw;* Copland: *Nonet, Statements,* and *Dance Symphony;* Stravinsky: *Abraham and Isaac, Orpheus, Octet,* and *Rite of Spring*). Faber Music Ltd. (Britten: *Songs and Proverbs of William Blake*). Novello & Company Ltd. (Elgar: *Enigma Variations;* Holst: *The Perfect Fool*). Peters Edition (Cage: *Music of Changes* and *Water Music;* Cardew: *Treatise* and *Octet '61;* Morton Feldman: *Intersection No.3*). Punch office (a sketch from *Punch* dated 30.11.66). United Music Publishers Ltd. (Ed. Alphonse Leduc, Paris — Messiaen: *Chronochromie.* Ed. Le Chant du Monde, Paris — Milhaud: *Quartet No.8*). Universal Edition (London) Ltd. (Bedford: *That white and radiant legend;* Cardew: *Four Works;* Lumsdaine: *Kelly Ground*). Universal Edition (Alfred A. Kalmus) Ltd. (Bartók: *Quartet No. 3;* Berg: *Chamber Concerto* and *Lyric Suite No.4;* Boulez: *Pli selon pli* and *Structures I;* Bussoti: *Piece for David Tudor;* Haubenstock–Ramati: *Credentials;* Janáček: *Aus einem Totenhaus;* Kagel: *die Reihe No. 7* and *Transicion II;* Mahler: *Symphony No. 2;* Moran: *4 Visions, No. 2;* Schoenberg: *Pierrot Lunaire* and *Third Quartet;* Stockhausen: *Klavierstück I, VI,* and *X, Kontakte, Kreuzspiel, Studie II,* and *Zyklus;* Webern: *Gleich und Gleich*).

Preface

Points of view

Go into any big music library, and you will find, on the shelves marked 'Notation', books on a great many apparently disconnected subjects. There are detailed and learned studies of notations of other cultures and ages (and particularly of the Middle Ages). There are practical textbooks, describing in more or less detail the established 'rules' of conventional notation, often including useful information on layout of parts, even choice of ink, nibs, and paper. There are always a few older books, generally slim, often privately printed at the author's expense, suggesting reformed systems which are to replace all the established ones. There are well produced books on today's avant-garde notations, exclusively concerned with the latest developments. Only two groups of writers seem to show interest in the general principles on which notations are formed, or the ways in which notations reflect the needs and preoccupations of users. These are the avant-gardists, who tend to look on all questions from their own reforming viewpoint; and, less predictably, the ethnomusicologists – whose writings have to be sought out in another part of the library.

This generally accepted view of 'Notation' as comprising a number of separate, specialized, studies of generally fixed and static systems, has led to the idea that anything written about the subject is likely to be technical, dry, and of little interest to non-specialists. Yet if we consider the established pattern of Western musical activity – in which A tells B what he is to do for the benefit of C – it is clear that the whole process depends on the choice of a suitable notation to serve as a link between A and B; one which will both express what needs to be expressed and allow information to flow smoothly between the two. Whether we have special or general interests, I do not see how we can know too much about the workings of the system, and the nature of this essential link. Practical musicians, who already use the systems confidently and fluently, may be sceptical about the value of a general study of notation, and could add that we are stuck with the system anyway and there is not much we can do about it. Yet

I

to use the system confidently and fluently is not necessarily to use it to best advantage. Agreed that we can make it work for us – would it work better if we were more fully aware of its mechanisms, its potentialities, its limitations? How does a notation's structure relate to the jobs we ask it to perform? In what fields can we express our requirements in precise terms? How much is left unsaid? When something is left unsaid, is this out of necessity or by intention? How is responsibility shared between sender and receiver? How far does adequate realization depend on the goodwill of the performer, or on reflex, subconscious reaction? These are the sorts of question we need to answer if we are really to understand the system in depth. On the second point – while fifty years ago we might reasonably have thought ourselves to be stuck with the system for better or worse, today, change is in the air. Conventional notations are showing the strain as the range of interest extends far beyond conventional time-pitch relationships; composers and performers are beginning to realize that a notation may make assumptions, in its forms and uses, about the nature of the musical game, and the relationship between the players of the game, that may be inappropriate to the new activities which they envisage.

The aim of this book, then, is to examine the role played by notations in the whole complex of current activities which we lump together as 'music'. It deals with systems, but the emphasis is on the ways in which we use them, and the situations which produce them, proceeding on the assumption that it is more important to describe how symbols *are* used than to direct how they *ought* to be used.

If we take notation, in this wider sense, to include the whole context of use, the subject becomes less manageable, its boundaries merging in every direction with those of related studies; but it is also enriched, involving as it does so many aspects of musical thought and activity that concern all music-lovers. For as we relate notations to the situations and circumstances in which they operate, they can be seen to act as barometers which register changes and fluctuations in the musical climate, reflecting the divisions and uncertainties of the age, the preoccupations, prejudices, and inter-relationships of their users. Every age, you could say, gets the notations it deserves – and perceptive study should lead us, not simply to an understanding of the structure and syntax of notations themselves, but to a clearer view of the structure of the musical culture within which they operate, and of the ways in which our modes of thought are influenced by the nature of the systems we use.

The rules and codifications of rudiments books and traditionally organized grammars may be convenient aids for beginners, and represent the actual state of affairs not too badly in ages when respect for tradition stands high and when rates of evolution are slow. In times of rapid change, the rules are everlastingly out of date; nor can any rigid, self-contained system that seeks to establish 'correct' and 'incorrect' usages, or to fix a principle of 'one sign one meaning', allow for the infinite number of variations of meaning that arise in the context of use Actual uses arise without regard for the laws of syntax or etymology*; to seek to fix meanings for notational symbols precisely and for ever is as unrealistic as to declare that screwdrivers are only to be used for driving screws – most of us also use them, quite successfully, to open paint tins or to remove stones from the heels of our shoes. In like manner, writers and composers take the tools of their trade (words, sounds, or notational symbols) and use them, freely and imaginatively, according to the needs of the moment. We have only to turn to actual working situations to discover that the ways in which notational symbols are used are as varied, subtle – often as unpredictable – as the uses of the written word.

Scope
This book is concerned with uses of notation in the Western world today, and the historical background is only briefly sketched in.

* Two examples, one non-musical, one musical, will illustrate the gap between 'correct' and actual uses. Someone wrote to the London *Daily Mirror* asking a favourite columnist to settle a difference of opinion that had arisen. Was the correct phrase 'one fell swoop' or 'one foul swoop'? The columnist duly enlightened the writer – but if he and his friends had gone on saying 'one foul swoop' to each other, the words would have served just as well.

The rudiments books are still declaring that beamings follow the rhythmic divisions of music according to historical precedent, and engravers are still 'correcting' the beaming of such revolutionaries as Brahms, who used beams to indicate the manner of articulation.

No attempt is made to guide the reader in the interpretation of music of past ages – in this field, only close and detailed study and actual use can lead to a true understanding; for this reason I have thought it best to leave the whole subject alone. Notations before Beethoven's lie outside the present range, though I have used them in places for comparison. In thus narrowing the field, a considerable benefit is lost. Historical and musicological studies are valuable, not only for their intrinsic interest, but as offering a route of escape from the tyranny (unfelt but always present) of the too-familiar systems of the present day. Yet today there are other routes of escape from the cage of our own traditional symbolisms. The needs of ethnomusicologists, electronic and avant-garde composers, force them to take account of the limitations and presuppositions of conventional notation. I hope that the discussion of specialist notations in these fields will help the reader to broaden his ideas as to what constitutes a note, an interval, or a rhythm, as effectively as yet another rush through the medieval neumes, the subdivisions of Time and Prolation, or seventeenth-century ornament notations.

Any approach that involves actual uses leaves the field wide open; a bar-by-bar commentary on Beethoven's op. 130 or Stravinsky's *Rite of Spring* would reveal unnumbered subtleties of use. Clearly, one has to stop somewhere. I have tried here to indicate the main types of notational problem, and the possible solutions, rather than to produce an encyclopedia of notational practice. I have not covered the conventions of layout: such matters as when stems go up or down; when slurs go over the heads of the notes; whether, at a change of clef, the new clef comes before or after a rest. Nor have I attempted a compendium of specialist notations. You will not find here special signs for six sorts of trumpet mute, or for plucking harp strings in unlikely ways and places. Even so, the general reader may prefer to skip lightly over some of the technicalities in the second and third parts.

The extended discussion of the communication situation and of reading processes may seem, to some, out of place in a book on notation. In my view, they represent essential aspects of the notational complex. Expression and communication are the two sides of a single coin; we need to know not only how signs represent sounds, but how they are understood and acted on. The notator must be able to put himself in the position of the receiver of the message; to know why a particular style and manner of communication is appropriate in some circumstances and not in others; to anticipate the difficulties that may arise in the heat and stress of performance. The most successful notators always have a keen sense of the situation at the receiving end of the line. This is why professional copyists, specialists in performer-reaction, are so often expert judges of the potentialities and limitations of the medium.

The great proliferation of experimental notations in recent years raises problems. It is clearly impossible to include all the new signs and inventions—many, too, are specifically designed as 'once only' notations, and will retain our interest for just as long as we care to listen to the works in which they appear. I have tried to make a meaningful selection, choosing examples to illustrate main lines of development and ignoring many interesting and original experiments. Wherever possible, I have taken examples from scores that are generally available at not too impossible prices.

Acknowledgements

In addition to the copyright owners mentioned on p. vi I am very grateful to Dennis Fry, professor of Experimental Phonetics at University College, London, for advice on the chapters on the communication situation; to Tristram Cary, Peter Zinovieff, and Nicholas Zvegintzov, who have read or discussed with me the section on electronic music, and who have lent me material or introduced me to working computers; and to the staffs of many libraries on whose resources I have drawn – and particularly that of the University Library, London.

PART ONE The Background

1 *Origins and Uses of Musical Notation*

Origins

Little is known about the origins of musical notations – not only because information is lacking, but because much has still to be sifted. (In China, where the earliest known notations date from before A.D. 100, 23,000 tons of bone, tortoiseshell, and bronze inscriptions wait to be deciphered before we can trace their origins.) In all cultures of which we have knowledge, however, word literacy has preceded music literacy. In all these cases, models existed for the formation of written symbolic scripts. For this reason there is no parallel with the slow evolution of word writing through picturegraphs, ideographs, syllabic writing, to the alphabetical system – that far-fetched process in which we chop up meaningful sounds into the smallest distinguishable units. meaningless in themselves, which are represented by *letters*.* The earliest known musical notations are constructed on the alphabetic principle of 'one sound (or pitch) – one symbol'. In most cultures that have developed notations,[1]however, we find many notations simultaneously in use and can trace the prototypes of most of the notational methods that are still in use today. The main systems can be listed as:

1) Alphabetic notations, using words, syllables, or letters to stand for single sounds of fixed pitch.
2) Directional signs, to indicate rising or falling pitch.
3) Group signs, to indicate melodicles – recurring groups of notes that always appear in a set form.
4) Tablatures: action notations which lead the player's fingers to the required place on his instrument.

The earliest known notations are theoretical rather than practical. Greek theorists were concerned to define scales that reflected

* The sound units themselves are technically called 'phonemes'.

6

an ideal, abstract order based on principles of number mysticism, and to establish connections between the allied arts of music, mathematics, geometry, and astronomy (the Quadrivium of the Ancient World). In China, theorists were concerned with the *correct* fixing of pitches for the degrees of the scale; on this correctitude was thought to depend the welfare of the nation. 'If the preceding government had been unsatisfactory in any way, or if there had been epidemics, droughts, or other diseases, it was the duty of the new Emperor and the Imperial music office (a branch of the office of weights and measures) to improve matters by revising the basic musical sounds in fixing the pitch of the huang-chung.'[1] In both Greece and China, it seems probable that the connection between theoretical and official scales and tunings, and the actual practice of performing musicians, was tenuous, where it existed at all.

Many early directive notations were teaching aids rather than instructions to the performer – directions, that is, at second hand. Teachers transmitted instructions orally, or by gesture, as appears in this description of the use of Byzantine cantillation signs: 'The domestikos, who could be seen by all, directed the singers with the movements of his right hand and with certain gestures; raising, lowering, extending, contracting, or putting together his fingers, and instead of the musical signs he formed the various melodic groups and inflections of the voices in the air. And everyone watched the leader of the choir and followed, one might say, the structure of the whole composition.'[2] The notations of Chinese lute teaching books were also meant for teachers to use; masters were not at all anxious to transmit their secret skills too widely, and the last chapter of didactic lute books was often omitted for this reason.

One broad distinction can be made between the uses of notation in East and West. Eastern notations, from their origin to the present day, have been used either to provide an outline to be filled in by improvising performers, or to set up the rules and conditions for performance without charting an exact course. Western notations have increasingly reflected a view of music as a closely planned activity. Considerable latitude may, at different periods, have been allowed and taken: in the elastic tempo notations of the thirteenth century; in the figured basses and melodic lines (that demand ornamentation) of the eighteenth; in the indeterminate music of our own day, and the 'basic' piano conductor scores of hit tunes which band-leaders use as a starting-point for arrangement and improvisation. But the general tendency has been in the direction of fixing the course of performance ever more exactly, detail by detail.

In one point, however, all notations from earliest beginnings almost to the present day find common ground. Durations, timbre, inflection, mode of attack, may or may not be specified by the notational directive at different times and places. But all notations have been concerned to specify pitch, or the relationship of pitches. For the conscious disinterest in pitch-relationships shown by some of today's composer-notators, there is no historical precedent.

Areas of interest in a musical culture are reflected in its notations. In the West, we have developed exact time-pitch specifications, but in other respects have never attained the subtlety or degree of detail shown in notations of certain types of Eastern music. Where our traditional notation has just one way of indicating the rising interval of a second, the Byzantine cantillation system has six, each sign corresponding to a different way of passing from note to note; as well as two independent signs for the descending second:

Ascending second

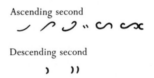

Descending second

Our *pizzicato* is unspecific compared with the precise instruction given in Chinese lute tablatures as to the manner in which a string is to be plucked – with which finger; whether inward or outward:

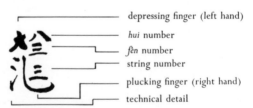

depressing finger (left hand)

hui number

fên number

string number

plucking finger (right hand)

technical detail

In some teaching notations, twenty-six varieties of vibrato may be distinguished, while elaborate instructions for performance-preparation (specifying, for instance, the exact number of silken threads from which each lute string is to be composed) seem to anticipate contemporary concern with action as an end in itself, sound as an incidental product.

We should, then, be very cautious in attributing lack of analytical or intellectual capacity to notators of other times or cultures if their notations fail to correspond to our own standards of selectivity or precision in certain directions. To arrive at a notation system at all implies a far from primitive outlook; Greek and Chinese theorists seem in fact to have been characterized by no lack of analytical capacity, and by intellectual over-activity rather than incapacity. Many difficulties were brought on by the excessive elaboration of theoretical scales and systems that bore little relationship to actual playing or singing situations. Nor can the existence of 'pormanteau signs' such as the Byzantine cantillation signs mentioned above, that offer an unfamiliar way of combining directives (pitch rise *plus* manner of passing from note to note), be taken as a sign of a primitive outlook, or of inability to distinguish pitch as a separate element. It would be truer to say that the Byzantines were led to pack their portmanteaus in a different way from ours, in which the time-pitch symbol displaces all other possible combinations.

Uses

The evolution of notational uses runs parallel to the evolution of forms and structures. All earlier notations seem to have shared the common purpose of preserving and safeguarding the music of a culture, whether by defining a theoretical basis, establishing the course of ritual performance, or by transmitting performing skills or the rules of the musical game. Later uses, which have evolved over the last thousand years, and mainly in the West, can be briefly listed:

1) To allow the writer to invent new music, and to calculate effects in advance and at leisure.
2) To provide an exact timetable, so that independent parts may be closely co-ordinated.
3) To provide the performer with an artificial memory.
4) To describe the sounds of performed music for purposes of analysis or study (as, for instance in the notations of folk-music collectors).

With these uses, and their effects on the nature and development of Western music, we shall be largely occupied in this book. It is probably safe to say that all were totally unforeseen by the early users of notational scripts. They could no more have foretold

9

them than an eighteenth-century composer could have foretold the use of notation to protect copyright.* As has so often happened in the history of technologies, inventions designed for use in one field have found their widest application in other, unrelated fields.

2 *Communication in General*

This chapter deals with the workings of communication systems in general; the ways in which the forms and structures of systems are related to uses, and some of the general problems with which users of musical notations are concerned. (A more detailed discussion of the nature and characteristics of the present day system follows in the next chapter.) This discussion of communication will lead us rather off the main track; but it is essential to understand something about the general nature and modes of use of the tools of communication before going on to the particular systems and uses developed by literate musicians in our own day.

The nature of sounding languages
All languages are selective. They work with a limited range of sounds, and pay attention only to certain aspects of those sounds. In speech, we use only a tiny fraction of the possible range of mouth-noises available to us, and attend only to the buzzings, hummings, explosive or voiced sounds that we recognize as con-

---

* *Ussachevsky has described how unwillingly he spent 40 hours producing a score of his 'Piece for Tape Recorder', to protect the work's American copyright.*

sonants and vowels in a given language by which primary meaning is conveyed. Pitch, duration, and intensity are not, in Western speech, vehicles of primary meaning. That is to say, we can say 'shut the door' loudly or softly, fast or slow, high or low, and the primary meaning remains unchanged. Only the essential language-sounds, the vowels and consonants, must be recognizably articulated. In traditional Western music, primary meaning lies in pitch and time relationships, and in these alone. That is to say, you can play 'God save the Queen' staccato or legato, loudly or softly, on trombone or penny whistle, and primary meaning remains unchanged; the tune remains itself. But you tamper with its time or pitch relationships at your peril.

Written scripts
Word and music notations follow the structure of the sounding languages they represent. Letter symbols represent the sounds we call consonants and vowels; note-symbols specify pitches and durations. We can, and do, make use of double notations, which reflect the way in which our attention is directed at the time of use. In the example below two independent sound-languages are in simultaneous use, and the two notations, each with its own terms of reference, reflect our double interest: verbal and musical.

God   save   our   grac – ious Queen

Notations such as these are special purpose tools, and their areas of interest overlap at no point. In Chapter One, the point was made that 'areas of interest of a musical culture are reflected in its notations'. This statement is true in a particular as well as a general sense. The familiar time-pitch graph shown above reflects in its structure, and uses, the rules of our own particular musical game, in which, conventionally, there are just twelve notches in the octave wall of sound, and in which durations stand in simple multiple relations to one another. Change the game, and the notation must change too. Our notation could never serve for a music in which interest centred on mode of attack, or in which the expressive force lay in the way in which each note was joined to the next, or in which a mechanically divided scale was used (as, for example, the scale of Turkish zither music, where the intervals are defined as the twenty equal divisions of the finger-board).

It could tell us little about the real nature of semi-improvisatorial Eastern music—and least of all (since it concerns itself with relationships between notes rather than the quality of individual notes) about the gong and lute musics of Ancient China, where the flavour of every sound has to be savoured separately: 'each note an entity in itself, calculated to evoke in the hearer a special reaction'.[3]

Interaction

We have said that written scripts and notations reflect the sounding languages they represent; but this statement needs qualification. In the first place, though written languages evolve, they have a natural tendency to conservatism and change at a slower rate than the sounding languages. This is why there is often so wide a gap between the pronunciation and the spelling of living languages. The spellings of today's English, it has been said, represent the pronunciations of four or five hundred years ago. Printing has strengthened the tendency towards the standardization of spelling and letter- and note-forms; but the fact that symbols retain their familiar look is no guarantee that their connotations remain unchanged. 'Outward and visible signs remain: they take over new content and meaning under new conditions. Our world would crumble if this were not so.'[4]

We should remember too, that in a literate society there is two-way action between sounding and written languages. The influence of spelling upon sounds in modern English has decided the pronunciation of many words: 'Spelling pronunciations become more frequent day by day. Pope rhymed "join" with "line", but it was a foregone conclusion that the historical pronunciation of *join* would not hold out for very long against the pull of the spelling.'[5] And similarly in music, notations help to decide the ways in which we perceive and pronounce sounds. We are encouraged, for instance, to hear and perform a tune as a succession of notes strung together like beads on a string, because notation tells us 'this is how tunes are made'. Non-literate jazz musicians have none of the literate musician's inhibitions about free use of glissando and portamento: it is our veneration for the urtext that leads us to the attitude that 'whatever is not in the score must be wrong'.

The influence of the structure of language and notations on the modes of thought of users is profound but immeasurable. By its structure, any system limits development in certain directions;

with the Roman number system it was impossible to do complicated accounts or to find the square root of VII. The structure of our own conventional notation system has similarly influenced the course of musical evolution – by encouraging us to think of music exclusively in terms of pitch and time relationships and by discouraging us from notating microtones or irregular rhythms. (The difficulty of notating a precisely timed accelerando, which is all but impossible in conventional notation, will be discussed later.) Conversely, a new notational technique may open the way to new ways of thinking about music. But it is rarely possible, in such matters, to be dogmatic about cause and effect. Did the evolution of precise mensural notations lead to the elaborate polymetric motets of the Netherlands School, or were the notations evolved to meet felt but inarticulate needs? Would avant-garde composers of our own day have written so much metreless music if they had not been attracted by the simplicity and logic of proportionate time notations?

Natural and artificial systems
The word and music languages so far discussed belong to the group of natural (open) systems; they have achieved their present form by slow growth, shaped by the needs of users, and subject to no strictly defined rules of use. The written scripts of languages in this group resemble the languages themselves in that there are no fixed, inflexible rules for their use, and because symbols and connotations are liable to change as the sounding language changes. They evolve gradually, bearing upon them signs of former usages —vestiges of the past, inconsistencies forced on them by the need to adapt to new circumstances.

A second type of system is the artificial (closed) system, invented and self-consistent, in which the meaning of each term is fixed by definition. In this group come the symbol systems of mathematicians and chemists, the Morse Code, and the artificial computer languages of our own day. The use of these synthetic languages depends, of course, on their users abiding strictly by the rules of use. Scientists and mathematicians abide by the definitions of their symbolic languages, but in other, broader fields of use, and in situations which are themselves ill-defined, artificial systems will always be liable to modification. When the artificial language of Esperanto was introduced into the American mid-West, words began to take on new meanings, and irregular constructions soon crept into use. There are already dialects of artificial computer

13

languages, introduced by the manufacturers of different computers. Music, too, has its artificial languages in the self-consistent newly-invented systems of some avant-garde composers. But here, too, there is nothing to stop later users adapting the proposed systems to their own ends.

The idea that the ideal notation would be rigidly organized on the 'one sign – one meaning' basis of a scientific code is widely held among composers and writers on notation. Even Thurston Dart gives as one of the *essential rules* of any well-devised set of symbols that 'each symbol should only have one meaning'.[6] Yet symbols with a broad, ill-defined content of meaning have their uses in all organic languages and notation systems, their special advantage being that they allow for subtle shades of meaning that can never be suggested if connotations are rigidly fixed. 'If all . . . references were unique, no ambiguity would arise but the labour of specification would be so great that communication would be hopelessly restricted . . . the power to extend thought has to be purchased at the risk of ambiguity. This is the real reason why language is apt to mislead, and any attempt to make it foolproof will inevitably reduce its potency.'[7] In music, such signs as the staccato dot and the line have only vaguely defined meanings, and that is why they can be used in different contexts with so much subtlety.

It should also be remembered that notations are not often designed to be read at all times by all comers; they may well be used in a context where viva voce elucidation is available, or where local traditions of performance are known to all. What is ambiguous in a general context becomes unambiguous in a particular context. The rigidity of a notation should then depend on the situation. Scientific notations need to be precise, because a single misreading may invalidate a whole process; the fate of nations may hang on the precise interpretation of a word-message. In these cases words must be used as precision tools. In conversational situations, and in many music situations, ease of use and subtlety of inflection may make a freer, flexible approach appropriate and effective.

How directive signs operate
Symbols do not carry meanings as trucks carry coal . . . their function is to select from a given context.

(E.H. Gombrich)[8]

Written notation ... is primarily a guide to the well-schooled performer. In other words it is a sort of shorthand that provides the initiate with skeletal and more or less fragmentary information of a primary mnemonic character.

(T.C. Grame)[9]

The efficiency of a notation (or any directive system) has nothing to do with the completeness with which it 'describes' required sounds or actions. The function of the sign is to serve as a trigger to action: we feed a coin to the slot machine, which responds with chocolate; we feed the written note to the player, who responds with the required sound. The connection between stimulus and response is an arbitrary one, which we establish for our own convenience; all that matters is that we shall have agreed in advance that a certain sign shall stand for a certain action or complex of actions. The sign *selects a response*; it does not need to *describe* any more than the starter's pistol needs to describe the course of the race to be run.

What constitutes an adequate directive? The answer, of course, depends entirely on the situation at the receiving end. In known situations we dispense with lengthy specifications. To the ferry-man we say only 'pull for the shore'; we do not tell him how to row the boat. The architect specifies a standard fitting by quoting a reference number; he does not give full working drawings for every light switch or window catch. In the same way, the music-writer makes use of the skills, and behaviour patterns which the reader has already learnt, giving him as much information as he wants and no more. Where instructions are issued for all comers, a certain basic standard of skill and knowledge is presumed to exist,* whether in road sign systems, telephone booth instructions, or in the symbols of conventional notation. The assumption is that we already know how to drive a car, how to dial, or how to finger and blow our instruments. If we do not, then a special teaching notation must be used. If we think that a whole complex procedure is known to a performer, we need not, of course, do more than indicate which procedure we want him to follow. Thus, for a concert pianist, we could simply specify a particular sonata and

---

* Though all systems will be too difficult for some users. Dr. R. Conrad (of the Applied Psychology Research Unit at Cambridge) says of mass technological systems: 'Many . . . will not use them at all. There are people who will run two miles to fetch an ambulance rather than telephone; people who will not even venture on the Underground' (*The Listener*, 13 July 1967).

15

he could, if the work was in his repertory, at once give the right response. K537 then becomes a group-sign for the Coronation Concerto: not what we generally mean by a notation, but the difference from the score is only one of the amount of detail specified. In both, there is a mnemonic element. (The score of the concerto tells you nothing about the way in which you are to play the piano and assumes knowledge of a suitable 'tradition of performance'.) The appropriateness of a notational system has nothing to do with the completeness, incompleteness, or the amount of detail shown. It can only be determined in terms of the performer's ability to interpret it.

3 *Communication in Music*

Descriptive, directive, and theoretical uses in the modern world

When we come to consider modern uses of notation, we shall be chiefly concerned with directives. In practice, however, directive, descriptive, and theoretical uses of notation cannot be neatly separated off. The descriptive scores of ethnomusicologists, and the study scores of electronic music, produced after the event, are, it is true, pure descriptive notations, made to tell us how music has actually sounded, rather than to specify the way in which music shall be made to sound. But the conventional score, though primarily a directive, is really a double purpose article—both instruction book and record. The performer reads it as directive; the score-reader or conductor as description of hypothetical performance. The composer issues a directive, but from another point of view he is *describing* the sounds in his head. The score remains for him, as for the earliest notators, the storehouse of information, repository of the sacred text; and he will put into the score specifications more detailed than the immediate needs of performance warrant. Yet today, preservative functions of the score are relatively unimportant; record and tape have taken over the function of telling us how music really sounds. 'The only true notations are the sound tracks on the record itself', Bartók remarked, speaking of the difficulty of devising a satisfactory descriptive notation.

All notations, directive or descriptive, are also theoretical in so far as they express for us the grammatical structure of the music we hear or play, guiding us to a particular mode of understanding. If, for instance, during a broad rallentando, crotchets gradually expand in length till they are longer than minims at the original speed, the notation still holds us to our perception of the notes as 'members of the class of crotchets'. (So, at a circus, we might recognize a family of dwarves and a family of giants, while recognizing also that the largest dwarf was in fact taller than the smallest giant). There is, for the literate listener, a sort of double tune in performed music: a tension between the theoretical, ideal values established in the 'rules' of the language, and the real values of the notes as he hears them. It is the existence of the known law that makes possible the flexibility and freedom of wayward performances; that is to say, we can accommodate ourselves to the fluctuations of rubato in an expressive Chopin performance because we are assured in our minds and by the look of the notes on paper that there are still (ideally rather than actually) three beats in every bar.

Limitations of notational directives

The instructions on a packet of soup, or the directions for assembling a model aeroplane, can be successfully followed by any reasonably intelligent person to get an end-result that will be accepted as satisfactory. There are several reasons why it is almost impossible to give a notational directive in a manner that will *ensure* a satisfactory end-result for all potential users. The first reason is that the directive is necessarily incomplete on *essential matters*. In notating related durations and pitches we can arrange symbols in a rank order that corresponds, well enough for practical purposes, to the way in which we perceive them. We can also discriminate between degrees of loudness and arrange symbols to represent them, though here we can be much less specific. In other dimensions of sound (timbre, types of attack and articulation) no rank order can be established. In these fields, we can only tell the performer to follow a known course of action (if one exists) or suggest a model – as when we suggest a timbre by writing *flautando* above the notes of a violin part. In either case, the notator must rely on the goodwill of the performer, rather as the playwright relies on the goodwill of the actor and producer, to whom, lacking a complete notation for timing, gesture, and inflection, he necessarily delegates some of his authority. There is always, then, a certain vagueness as to the precise form that the realization will take.

We are all, nevertheless, skilled at acting on incomplete instructions or interpreting incomplete messages. The message of the astronaut is interpreted successfully in spite of atmospheric static; the smallest hint from the bidder is successfully interpreted by the auctioneer. But in these cases, there is a common aim and interest. In the case of composer and interpreter common interest cannot be assumed to exist. The relationship between the two is inherently a tricky one, laden with possibilities of misunderstanding. Hence such outbreaks as Honegger's 'Do you not find it odious that a creative musician should be obliged to pass through the filter of another musician who plays his works? In painting would a picture restorer allow himself to retouch the work?'[10] Too often (and most of all in an age of specialization), composer and performer neither understand nor wish to understand one another, and in these circumstances the vagueness of the directive becomes a serious problem.

Another difficulty in analyzing the working of the system comes from the fact that we have become so habituated to our normal manners of use that we are no longer aware of the ways in which we inflect and vary the terms of the directive. There is no such thing as a literal interpretation: we can no more follow the instructions precisely than we can pronounce the words of our own language without naturally and involuntarily introducing inflections of stress, pitch, rhythm, and intonation. There is an instinctive element in all interpretation: we know, perhaps, that we diverge, but are often unaware of the extent of divergence. This is one reason why the determinate notations envisaged by Stravinsky, Schoenberg, and Boulez (and discussed in Chapter 16) can never achieve their whole objective.

Characteristics of the conventional system
Three special circumstances in the familiar notational situation are influential in deciding the form of the message.

1) Notation imposes a variable time limit. We read a book at a speed which we decide for ourselves. We read notation *adagio*, or *presto*, according to the specification.
2) There is a progressive handing-over of responsibility to the performer as he carries out instructions as to pitch, durations, articulation, timbre, in that order.
3) Notation is a one-way directive, and so tends to adopt authoritarian rather than collaborative patterns of direction.

1) *The time factor*

Telegrams are written in terse, elliptical, telegraphese to save expense; newspaper headlines, for reasons of space. Traffic signs and notation symbols must give their message briefly because of the time factor. The systems must be constructed so that the message can be instantly read, under favourable or unfavourable conditions. It is these requirements that have produced a notation full of vivid graphical features, which owe their existence to the need to make immediate impact, and which retain basic simplicity. Note that we can set no absolute limit for the amount that may be put over. In slow movements, there is more time to read, so notations may be more detailed. The amount of rehearsal time available also affects the issue: if a work is to be prepared at length, a detailed notation may be appropriate; if sight-read, information must be kept to the minimum.

2) *Areas of control*

The notational situation resembles the road situation, in which we are faced with a number of directives, all apparently imperative, but which we interpret with varying degrees of freedom. On the road, we recognize that the advertisement telling us to 'buy X' is a ruse designed to bring X to our attention, demanding no action on our part; that the speed limit sign should be regarded with respect, but interpreted with some flexibility; that the red traffic light demands absolute obedience. So in music, we recognize the affective message of mood markings: *con amore* demands no specific action on our part. We feel free to adapt phrasing and bowing, with due regard to the context, within what we decide for ourselves are 'reasonable limits'. Pitch and time specifications we obey literally, or at least keep within bounds that preserve the identity of pitch or time intervals as set forth in the score. The notation of time and pitch, as was suggested in the first section of this chapter, seems to represent ideal values which must always remain discernible through the vagaries of performance; though even here, an absolutely literal obedience is neither expected nor desired. Many of the player's activities are 'controlled', not by the notation, but by a broad mutual understanding as to what 'normal' behaviour consists of. The absence of timbre notation does not imply that the performer is free to play with any sort of tonal quality as long as he observes the specified pitch and time values, but that he will conform to the accepted standard of 'normal' tone-quality. It is the exceptions – con sordino, con legno, non vibrato – that need to be indicated. (So, in traffic situations, only the exceptional one-way streets need to be sign-posted.)

Identical symbolizations imply different degrees of permissiveness in different contexts. The jazz player will bend and modify time and pitch in note sequences in ways that would be wholly unallowable for the straight player. The eighteenth-century specialist doubles dots, plays quavers unequally, adds a scale and trill at the cadenza, in accordance with the terms of the unwritten contract. We can, in fact, only speak in a general way of 'areas of control'; they are subject to continual revision and variation, and only knowledge of the local situation tells us what is or is not allowable. Habitual patterns of response, slowly established and reinforced by use, and in which an unconscious reflex element is involved, cannot be instantaneously modified by the issuing of fresh directives. Though we can (on paper) extend the area of control or allow new freedom into the score, we cannot impose the attitudes needed, if the new directives are to be effectively carried out. Orchestras brought up in the romantic tradition of free tempo variation find the greatest difficulty in interpreting highly determinate scores of Stravinsky or Boulez. To relax the pattern of literal obedience is just as difficult – German orchestras have gone on strike rather than accept the (to them) impossible situations of indeterminate music. But the commonest response to the directive that cuts across the established pattern of behaviour is to ignore it. 'A choice of method or direction of communication which is not in keeping with the existing pattern of organization within which it takes place does not mean that the pattern of organization changes to suit the method chosen. Usually it means that the method of communication has to be changed to suit the pattern of organisation.'[11]

20

3) *Notation as a one-way directive*

All written directives are one-way communications, and have to use authoritative rather than collaborative methods of instruction. In music, where very fine shades of meaning have to be conveyed, steps have to be taken to counteract the effects of uninvolved performance. First, the message can be expanded to the point where literal obedience will give adequate results even without understanding on the performer's side. This way leads to the highly determinate notations of the last fifty years. Next, special efforts may be made to help the player to an understanding of the music he is playing by supplementary markings that have no practical application (beaming, phrasing, mood-indications may come into this class). A third possibility is to involve the player by use of incomplete, paradoxical, or indeterminate notations, so that he is forced to take a collaborative part if he is to play the music at all. This is the method adopted by many of today's avant-garde composers.

With one-way communication, there is no feedback from performer to writer. Unclear directives cannot be questioned; the writer cannot check that instructions are adequately carried out: hence the need to guard against possible misunderstandings with extra care. Notation is full of redundancies, precautionary markings, and duplicated instructions (the chapters on pitch, dynamics, and silence will provide many examples). These built-in checks are particularly necessary in an age of specialization, when direct contact between composers and performers is often non-existent.

4 *Response: How we read Music*

Eye movements

How does the fluent player read the written note or word? Does the eye move across the page steadily or in jumps? How often does it regress or look ahead? How much does it take in at a glance? How is it that the expert can respond confidently and accurately to the complex and detailed instructions that spring up at him from the page of a Bach five-part fugue, or a Chopin scherzo? Such questions cannot be answered by introspection; the processes by which we scan and read lie hidden deep in our involuntary reflexes, and in the secret places of the subconscious mind. But a good deal of experimental work has been done on word-reading processes, from which we can piece together a fairly clear picture of the situation, as it involves the music-reader.

Eye movements were first studied by the desperate expedient of sticking bristles in plaster cups on to the cornea and recording movements direct onto a smoked drum; later, and more comfortably, by photographic methods. Reading takes place in the 'fixations' between jumps (saccadic movements); the length of fixation periods and the span of the visual field vary little between individuals, and do not increase with improved reading performance. The limit lies in the amount that can be comprehended at each fixation, rather than in the visual capacity. 'The organism has a definite limit for information which is a minute fraction of the contents of the physical signals that reach the eyes . . . the redundancy is enormous.'[12] All of us see more than we can possibly comprehend at each fixation. The good reader can get on by larger leaps because he takes in more; in the case of the slow reader, there is more overlapping between spans, so that a word-group or note-group may receive attention in several consecutive fixations.

Regression (backward fixation) occurs in all reading, though good readers make fewer regressions than slow readers. Attempts to control eye movements and inhibit regression do not lead to more efficient reading; there are no 'good' patterns of eye movements; quick readers are those who have developed a flexible method of approach, and who are ready to seize on essential clues to the sense, as and where they appear.

Comprehension

The fluent reader passes over letters, and even words, in favour of larger meaningful units. 'There is a hierarchy of recognition habits; the recognition of dominant parts of the word touch off the recognition of the total form; and similarly the recognition of a phrase *as* a phrase is achieved by the partial inhibition of the recognition of constituent words or letters in favour of the total recognition of the larger unit.'[13] When we read our own language, we recognize familiar word-profiles, pick up clues as to function and structure of sentences from characteristic successions of letters or words. We recognize grammatical situations as we recognize faces – not by this or that detail, but on an over-all basis. The same process applies in music reading. We read by chord profiles, by spotting parallels and sequences, regular scale and arpeggio passages; by our knowledge of the idiom and the likely outcome of the melodic or harmonic train of events. Good readers are those with a good stock of parallel situations, and the flexibility to vary reading speed and approach to meet each situation. Only the beginner spells out the music note by note – the expert will sight-read a passage, never pausing for missing barlines, dropped ties or notes, missing ledger lines; good orchestral players may use parts for years without discovering literal errors. It is, indeed, not easy for a fluent reader to put himself in a proof-reading frame of mind, taking note of every symbol. 'Practised newspaper and novel readers' William James wrote, 'could not possibly get on so fast if they had to see accurately every single letter of every word they read in order to perceive the words. More than half the words come out of their minds, and hardly half from the printed page.'[14] But notice that William James specifies easy, familiar types of text that lend themselves to quick reading. New or unfamiliar modes of thought or construction at once slow the process down. We read quickly when there is a high degree of predictability, and consequently a high degree of redundancy in the text; we hardly need the score to tell us that if the last chord but one of a piece is 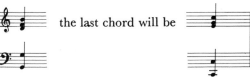 the last chord will be

Together with the power of reading through symbols to the meaning behind, the experienced performer has highly developed ability to traverse rough ground. Illegible symbols, badly formed accidentals, badly placed notes, will be rightly interpreted because he reads by context rather than by detail. We have little difficulty in interpretating hastily written manuscript as long as the idiom is familiar. Even where symbols are as widely written as in the Janáček autograph shown here, we may still be able to give them a meaning:

The performer will always grope for sense. If it is in the least possible, he will establish a meaning (if not always *the* meaning) as the letter-reader does:

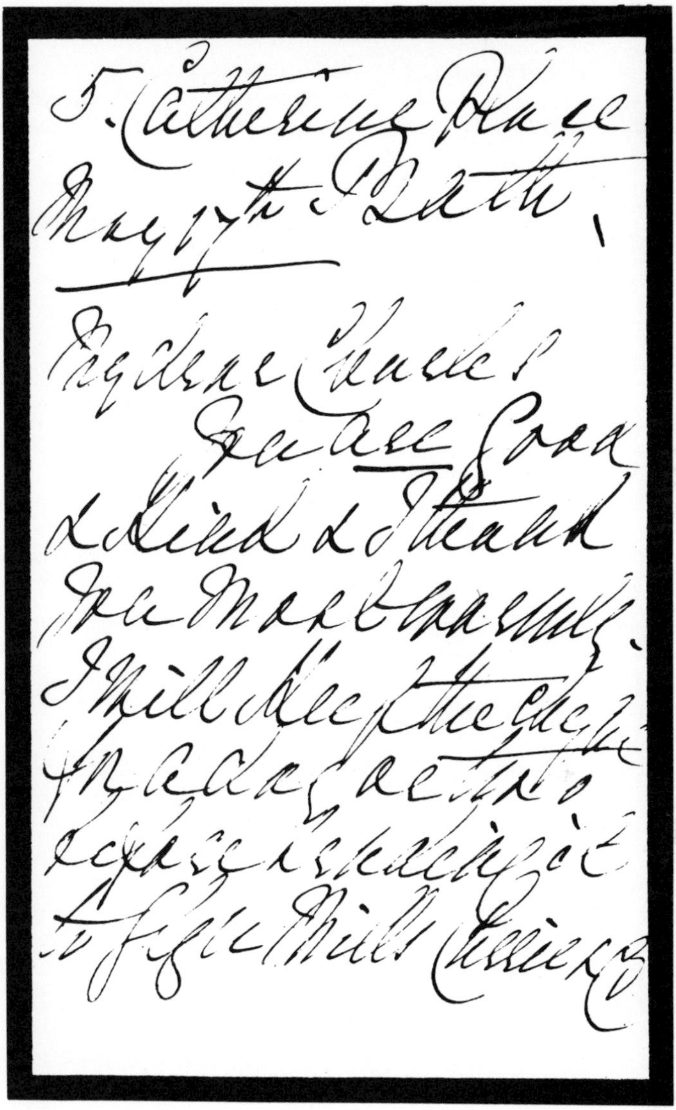

5. Catherine Place

May 17th Bath

My dear Charles?

In word reading, we adapt our speed to the difficulty of the text. In performance, we are tied to a set speed; but because the eye is not bound to move at the pace of the fingers, it can range on ahead, to collect information fractionally in advance of the moment when it is needed, so that there is generally a small reserve of time available. Anyone who has turned pages for good sight-readers will know how early they demand their turns – the eye is always several steps ahead of the fingers. One of the great advantages of the graphical features on the notational map is the advance warning that we get of the approximate density, direction, and type of movement from a single glance at the bars ahead. The score provides both a graphical sketch map and a detailed symbolic representation of the music simultaneously.

Standardization

'Loo, what should a man in thyse days wryte, aggs or eyren: certainly it is hard to please every man, by cause of the dyuersite & chaunge of langage.'

(William Caxton, 1490)

However charming and expressive we find the haphazard phonetic spellings of Elizabethan texts, or the first stories of young children, we submit in everyday life to standardization, without which characteristic letter and word shapes, note-symbols, and chord-profiles, would never be recognized. We tend to think of the changes, brought about by the invention of printing, in terms of the side dissemination of texts; but hardly less significant are the quick-reading, text-skimming processes made possible by letter and word uniformity. Even today, a high proportion of the scores, and parts in practical use need to be produced by hand and it is therefore essential that manuscript writers aim at the highest attainable degree of standardization and self-consistency. The wide and continued use of handwritten working scripts is an important limiting factor in the development of symbols. It remains essential that they should be easily, quickly, and unambiguously formed; a script that is laborious to write and easy to read would be unacceptable for economic reasons, while a script that is easy to write and hard to read would, obviously enough, be unacceptable for practical reasons. In fact, the basic symbols in the repertoire are few and very simple, and there is little variations between printed and manuscript forms (significant variants occur only in the case of the crotchet rest):

But   ♩   print =   ✓♩ manuscript crochet rests

Graphical and non-graphical notations

The undoubted advantages of graphical notations as an aid to quick reading in conventional situations should not lead us to jump to the conclusion that further extensions of the principle will necessarily lead to more efficient use, or that the pretentiously described 'psycho-visual' truth of a notation is all that is important to understanding use. We have no difficulty in getting at the meaning behind arbitrary letter-symbols, even though there is no correspondence between symbols, and objects or ideas represented by the symbols. 'Our whole life, indeed, is structured by our powers to establish cross-connections between our different modes of perception – as when we recognize the smell, the look, the feel, the spoken or written name of an object, as aspects of a single entity. The advantages of pictographic symbolisms should, then, be assessed in practical terms: do they provide a clearer or more precise directive, or one that can be acted on more quickly, or by more people?

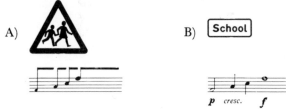

Above, sign A may well be useful to more people than sign B, which can only be read by English speakers; notation A carries no corresponding advantage, since all Western musicians can read conventional notation if they can read at all. Nor is there any reason to think that proportionate notations necessarily help us to a more intelligent or understanding interpretation. Their real valued lies in breaking through the habitual stimulus-response pattern, doing away with a whole unwanted tradition of interpretation.

27

5 *The Psychology of Notation*

Conventions of behaviour

We instinctively shrink from eny chainge in whot iz familiar: and whot can be more familiar than the form ov wurds that we have written more times than we can possibly estimate?[15]

There is nothing wrong with the word and note examples above except that they look wrong. In notation, certain procedures survive simply because they feel comfortable and right to us, and because to change them would cause us emotional disturbance without bringing any corresponding advantage. Even the dropping of rests from empty bars (or the dropping of the bars themselves) as practised in modern scores can inflict a slight shock on the conventional reader. The practice of keeping to what looks right has produced some curious notational inconsistencies, such as the vestigial figured basses that persist in some eighteenth-century orchestral scores after the continuo instrument had vanished from the orchestra; or the sforzandi in the organ part of Beethoven's *Mass in D* (put in to match up with other bass instruments):

or the crook-changes in Strauss's horn parts, specified even when no time is allowed for the change, so that the player is forced into a new transposition.

Tones of voice

The first purpose of a notation is to put over the message clearly and concisely. Yet there are forms of address appropriate to different communication situations which often decide the form the communication takes. We talk in one way to the tax inspector, in another to our family. Those in authority (headmasters) have one tone of voice: those under authority (schoolboys) another. The tone of voice of the eighteenth-century score, cut to fit the performer and offered with respect, is very different from the tone of voice of Schoenberg or Stravinsky, whose notations presuppose a performer who places himself at the composer's absolute disposal. From this view, it can be suggested that the indeterminate scores of today, which leave so much to the performer's responsibility and offer the directive in such visually attractive and ingratiating forms, recognize the fact that the old autocratic attitudes (of giants speaking to pygmies) are no longer appropriate in an age when composer and performer so often share an intellectual level. There is also the economic factor to consider: those who write for captive orchestras (eighteenth-century court orchestras or today's radio orchestras) can afford to be peremptory. Those whose works are played by the performers' favour and grace may feel the need to address them in more conciliatory terms.

A characteristic of the notation of our own age lies in the variety or tones of voice that may be used. In situations where the composer writes for hypothetical performers rather than actual groups, an objective, impersonal tone of voice is apparent; while avant-garde scores, often written for select groups of known performers, allow themselves to be familiar, informal, full of in-jokes and references. We have today no clear, consistent, picture of the roles of composer and performer in the realization of music, and our uncertainty is reflected in our notations.

Visual association

A Bach fugue, a Beethoven slow movement, or a Messiaen piano piece declares itself visually before a note has been sounded. Even the house-styles of publishers can affect the reader's attitude; vocal scores set in moveable type suggest Victorian oratorio, while there was something about the look of Universal Edition, long before the days of avant-gardism, that went with all that was newest from Central Europe. Attitudes can be set in advance by a suitable choice of notation – unwelcome associations can be avoided, affiliation declared. Teachers know that the sight of a page of semiquavers can send the learner into a nervous rigor, and that it is good practice to notate children's pieces in crotchets and quavers, avoiding the terror-inspiring double beams.*

* In the seventeenth century, the theorist Georg Muffat was already warning performers against *horror fusae* – the alarm caused by the sight of double fusae (semiquavers).

29

Modern hymn-writers consciously avoid the conventional white look of tunes written in minims and semibreves, and give their music a secular, up-to-date appearance by notating in crotchets and quavers. Alternatively, the associations of certain types of notation can be deliberately exploited – as in Britten's *Turn of the Screw*, where Miles's little eighteenth-century piano piece is notated with eighteenth-century ornament signs:

We may place a work in context by choice of notation. Mendelssohn's uncertainty over the notation of his *Midsummer Night's Dream Overture*:

was perhaps an uncertainty as to where the work's affinities lay – with a Haydn-Mozart type finale, or with the more explicit brilliance of, say, Paganini's *Moto Perpetuo*:

Attempts to rationalize Beethoven's time-signatures and note-values, or to rebar contrapuntal music in accordance with word or melody accentuation will always be suspect. The choice of time-signatures and note-lengths is a highly personal affair involving practical, psychological, and aesthetic considerations. We *may* simplify reading processes – we may also iron out a whole pattern of inflexion or nuance which is built into the traditional notation, or suggest a new and alien attitude. Elliot Button's rebarrings* change the accentuation patterns of Beethoven's music:

Walter Goehr's rebarrings, in eliminating metre and leaving only stress-patterns, seem also to be saying 'Look! Monteverdi is as modern as Stravinsky':

* *System in Musical Notation* (Novello, 1920).

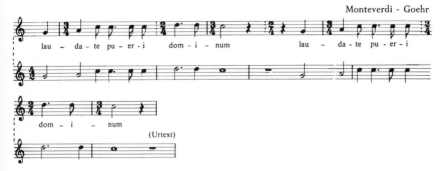

lau – da - te pu - er - i dom - i – num lau – da - te pu - er - i

dom – i – num

(Urtext)

The choice of appropriate note-values is to a large extent
governed by established conventions, but there is, perhaps, a
psychological element involved as well. We may ask why very
slow movements often appear notated in demisemiquavers and
hemidemisemiquavers (which we would expect to be short, fast
notes) while very quick movements may have quavers, or even
crotchets, for their shortest notes:

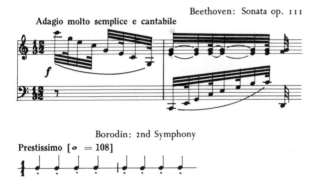

Beethoven: Sonata op. III

Adagio molto semplice e cantabile

Borodin: 2nd Symphony

Prestissimo [○ = 108]

Part of the explanation may be that the notation of fast movements in 'long' notes gives the impression of covering a great
distance at immense speed, while the much-divided beats of a
Beethoven Adagio suggest a music that puts time under the
microscope, examining each beat in minutest detail. A psychological reason can also be given for the appearance and disappear-
ance of ornament notations. In the eighteenth century, ornament
notation served to separate the decorative from the structural:
'Writing down graces', says Burney, 'is like rehearsing the non-
sense and impertinence of conversation, which, bad at first, is

31

rendered more and more insipid as the time and the manners which produced it become more distant.'[16] In the serious nineteenth century, once-accepted formulae turned into unacceptable clichés; every utterance had to be weighed, every statement had to be personal to the composer*. Where every note of every phrase is supposed to carry a serious meaning, decorative flourishes and conversational gambits have no place; and so abbreviation signs and ornament signs vanish from the vocabulary.

6 *Failures of Communication*

In this chapter, common causes of notation trouble are listed.

1) *Graphical faults* (poor spacing and alignment, badly-formed symbols, unclear layout).
2) *Inconsistency* (contradictory markings, symbols used in different senses without good cause).
3) *Too little information given* (that is, too little for adequate performance under the prevailing conditions).

These are common beginners' faults. Notes are badly formed and aligned; beaming, slurring, accent marks, are used without system; dynamics are incompletely marked; accidentals not cancelled. The most treacherous situation of all is that of the generally consistent writer who abandons consistency. If, for instance, *nearly* all simultaneous notes are properly aligned, the few exceptions will be much more likely to mislead than if alignment was haphazard throughout.

---

* Mahler's biographer, Kurt Blaukopf, provides an example of the attitude towards ornamentation of a great late-Romantic. When Mahler conducted Mozart, he would remove appoggiaturas and other ornaments, which he regarded as 'extraneous trimmings'.

4) *Too much information given* (that is, unnecessarily much under prevailing conditions).

5) *Meaningless precision.*

Composers who favour highly determinate notations are most likely to overload the channel, or give meaninglessly precise directives. 'Overloading' can only be relative to rehearsing and study time, as has already been stressed, but unnecessary instructions such as fingerings for expert players or bowings on every note are unnecessary in all conceivable contexts, and so unjustifiable. Excessive use of redundant and precautionary markings is also a symptom of overanxiety, and is to be deprecated.

6) *Uncertainty as to terms of contract* (degree of latitude to be taken in interpretation).

This occurs when players are not versed in the particular traditions of performance assumed by the notator. When music is written in many styles and on many different principles, the performer must know whether a strict, deadpan interpretation (as for Stravinsky) or a flexible, personal interpretation (as for Rachmaninov) is wanted. With new music, unconvincing first performances are often due to the performers not being able to guess how the work ought to go until they have heard it – and even then further explanation may be needed. The difficulties of interpreting older music are largely difficulties of deciding on the degree of latitude to be taken (and in which direction) in tempo, rhythm, dynamics, and articulation.

7) *Ambiguity* (where signs may have two meanings, only one of which can be right).

Genuine ambiguities (as opposed to 'historical ambiguities' – those created when a tradition of performance is forgotten) are not very common. Are celeste, glockenspiel, or horn in the bass clef, notated at pitch or an octave lower? Are slur marks to be read as bow changes or simply as phrase connections? Note that to allow latitude by using an indeterminate notation is not an ambiguity. The indeterminate sign says 'do A, B, or C, as you like'. The ambiguous sign can mean 'do A' or can mean 'do B', but cannot mean both.

8) *Insufficiency of notation for the job in hand.*

We may need and desire to notate things that cannot be notated, at least not with the system we use today. No adequate notation for timbre, modes of attack and decay, or controlled accelerandi has been evolved, and in these matters we cannot issue an adequate directive.

33

The examples below are chosen to illustrate some of these problems. It is suggested that the reader analyses these and tries to locate the probable cause of communication trouble before he reads the comments.

a)   Stravinsky: Orpheus

a) Line and dot (sustained, but not to full length), or Stravinsky's special mark for 'sharp attack without accent'? No explanation is given in the score.

b)

b) Characteristic beginners' faults, mainly of omission and inconsistency. There should almost certainly be a return to *arco* on the last beat of the first bar, and a *piano* is implied.

There must be some other mark before the *mf* in the third bar (last mark *f*). One of the two groups in the last bar must be a triplet. The turn is mechanically impossible.

c) Should the dotted rhythm of the piano be played as a triplet? A case of historical ambiguity, occurring at the critical moment when the convention was sometimes used, sometimes not used. This example was discussed at length in the *Musical Times* of September 1963: experts were evenly divided as to the answer.

d) Inconsistency of lines and accents; even in printed scores this type of inconsistent marking of homophonic passages is not uncommon.

* V.S.= Volti Subito (turn quickly).

34

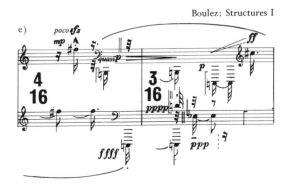

e) Unexplained *special signs*; meaningless crescendo; unrealizable range of dynamics (meaningless precision). On first note of right hand, double tautology (dot+semiquaver, accent+*sfz*). No realizable meaning for dot on last note of first bar.

f)

f) If this joke from *Punch* is funny, why is it so? Presumably because the notation is inappropriate – the monk is not concerned with the pitch of the bell or the exact number of times he is to ring it: the appropriate notation might be 'ring for five minutes'.

35

PART TWO The System at Work

This part of the book deals with the notation system as we use it today. Possible lines of approach are reviewed, and the uses of different systems in the present day context described. The rest of the section is given up to an anatomy and physiology of the system; a discussion, that is, of structure and functions, taken in order according to the different fields of specification – pitch, time-notation, etc.

Recent innovations are briefly discussed at the end of each section, but the more general account of experimental notations is held over till Part Three.

7 *Lines of Approach*

Units of dissection

In preparing or macerating a skeleton, the naturalist nowadays carries on the process till nothing is left but the whitened bones. But the old anatomists . . . were wont to macerate by easy stages; and in many of their most instructive preparations, the ligaments were intentionally left in connection with the bones, and as part of the skeleton.

(D'Arcy Thompson)[17]

The alphabet hacks the universal into visual segments.

(Marshall Macluhan)[18]

Music, because it is an art, provides us with an already created unity, a perfected *Gestalt*. To tear it to pieces in order to perceive it as such seems an irrational approach.

(James Mainwaring)[19]

Words, sentences, and melodic phrases, like living organisms, are meaningful wholes. Why should we need to anatomize living sounds into the letters of the alphabet, or the separate notes of conventional notation, when alternative methods are available?

By using picturegraphs, ideographs, group-signs of various types, meaningful units can be represented in scripts and notations.

Group-signs

GRAPHICAL   NON - GRAPHICAL

a) Road signs   (Picturegraphs)   (Ideographs)

Turn left   End of speed limit

b) Ornament notations

Ascending trill   Trill (modern)   A Shake   Trill (modern)
with turned ending.   (Purcell, 1696)
(Muffat, 1726)

c) Avant-garde group-signs
    Roger Reynolds: 'Quick are the
           Months of Earth'   Cardew: Octet, 61

There is, however, one very practical reason for the widespread use of one sound-one sign notations in the modern world. Ideographic notations can be used effectively only where the number of alternatives to be distinguished is small. In the limited traffic situation, or in the music situation of Byzantine chant, where 24 or so melodicles – small three or four-note units of unvarying shape – are joined in performance 'as a gardener arranges flowers',* the notation is appropriate to the activity. It is when the number of possible alternatives multiplies that a notation which demands a separate symbol for each course of action becomes unmanageable.† If we were to notate even every possible three-note com-

---

* 'The composer of cantillations, far from being a patcher, might better be compared to an ingenious gardener who arranges his two dozen of motley flowers in ever new bunches.' (C. Sachs)[20]
† The road sign situation has already arrived at the danger-point: at a recent census, 74% of drivers questioned thought that the 'no overtaking' sign meant 'you may now overtake'.

bination of our twelve-note scale by a separate symbol, we would need 1320 symbols. Ideographic notations have for this reason tended to become the exclusive property of priestly or learned sects. Laymen cannot hope to master the huge number of symbols used in Chinese ideographic writing, or in the ornament notation of the eighteenth century, aimed at the highly professional special-ist performer.‡ In the cryptic 'group-signs' of avant-garde nota-tions, we see a deliberate use of ideographs to forge a bond of understanding between composer and performer, a deliberate exclusiveness that limits use of the notation to those in the know.

Action notations

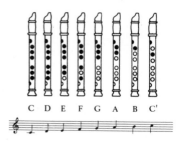

C   D   E   F   G   A   B   C'

This diagram, which could be taken from a 'First Recorder Book', shows one action notation and two sound-specifications. The advantages and limitations of the two types can be easily appreciated. The top systems tell you about the mechanics of recorder playing (but only if your instrument has English finger-ing) and nothing about the end-product. It would only be of use to a recorder player. The lower system tells you about the end product, but gives no help as to the means of obtaining it. It would tell as much to a violinist, a trumpeter, or a singer.

Action notations are only of use to instrumentalists. The singer must find his way to the right note by memory (if he has absolute pitch) or by assessing the relationship of each note to its neigh-bours. Only pitch or interval notations will serve his purposes.

‡ Ideographic notations in eighteenth-century music also served a secondary purpose. In representing 'ornaments' and 'graces' by group signs, the nota-tion sorted out structural from decorative elements, letting the player know what was cake, what was icing. (This is not to say that the icing could be dispensed with – it was often the reason for the cake's existence.)

Action notations need not be as cumbrous as the recorder chart shown here. Where only one finger has to be placed for each sounding note, a one sound-one sign notation results, intrinsically no harder to read or write than a conventional pitch-specifying notation. In the lute notation shown, the lines represent strings of the instrument and the finger-positions are given on a left-to-right time chart as in normal staff notation. Flagged stems appear whenever there is a change of time-value; letters refer to frets on the finger board, arranged at semitone intervals:

(Solution at end of chapter)

In modern guitar notations, each 'chord-box' provides a diagrammatic map of strings (vertical lines) and frets (horizontal lines) on which finger-positions for a particular chord are shown by dots:

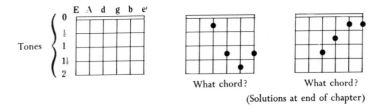

(Solutions at end of chapter)

Where musical activities remain separate within a culture, action notations may be widely used without their limited range of use being felt as a disadvantage. Seventeenth-century lutenists and present day guitarists have been happy enough with their private notations. When cultures have merged, the two types of notation have often continued in use side by side – or more accurately, above and below, as in sixteenth-century lute books (see Dowland example above); while today, guitar boxes appear together with conventional notations in folksong arrangements:

39

The main reason why action notations will never come back into wide use in the West lies not in their inadequacy or even in the versatility of performers who want to play many instruments. It lies in the fact that, once a notation of any sort has come into almost universal use, it is next to impossible to displace it.* It is essential to learn to read conventional notation if you are to have access to music written for practically any instrument (except the guitar). If a piano tutor were brought out tomorrow that did all it claimed to do in teaching its users to play from a number-notation in two weeks, it would still leave the user without access to the whole accumulated literature of piano music of the Western world. We are bound to conventional notation, efficient or in-efficient, as we are bound to our own language – because it is the accepted means of communication.

Action and sound-specifications combined

Although conventional notation is, basically, a specification of sounds to be produced, most scores provide examples of supplementary action notation. Certain special effects will be called for in terms of the action required (pizzicato, con sordino, sul G, etc.); bowings and fingerings are specified, practical instructions given (take piccolo, V.S.). The ways in which composers put across the directive are generally decided by the needs of the moment rather than by theoretical considerations. So, where parts are to be shared between hands in piano music we may find that the significant actions are indicated graphically even at the cost of obscuring the pitch-relationship map:

Bartók: Mikrokosmos 113

Modern experimental notations lean heavily on action description. The special effects obtainable from prepared pianos are only describable in terms of the nuts, bolts, or pieces of india-rubber used in the preparation. The philosophy of composers like Cage

---

* As the practical Dr. Burney realized when he wrote: 'Innovators will always find that a known method, however bad, will be preferred to the good method that is to learn.'

and Cardew, who attach as much importance to the activities of performance as the end-result in sound, leads naturally to a direct notation of action.

For the performer, the distinction between the two types of notation is of little significance. All symbols are to be read as incentives to action. Pianist, violinist, or flautist reading the sign ♪ will respond by placing fingers in the appropriate playing position, adjusting embouchure, etc. 'Middle C' will invariably signify both a playing position and the sound associated with it. Only the singer, who has no mechanical guide to action, is sure to use notation simply as a description of sounds (or their relationships); for him, each sound must be identified in the imagination before it can be produced.

Many conventional notations show an implicit recognition of the fact that it is often more useful to relate the notation to the player's actions rather than to the sounds he is to produce. The notations of transposing instruments simplify the player's task; every time the clarinettist sees the note C he will play the note *fingered* C on his instrument (which may sound as A, B flat, or E flat). The significance of the notation for him is, that is to say, 'one symbol position—one fingering' rather than 'one symbol position – one sound'. So too, string harmonics are conventionally notated according to their playing-positions (see p. 53).

Letter and number notations

The letters shown in the diagram on p. 38 are not always included in discussion of the notational complex; yet they deserve their place as labels of identification, which can be used to select a sound and action as distinctly as the symbols of pitch-specifying notations of more elaborate construction. Today, they are still indispensable as the call-words by which we can identify particular notes and clear up confusions *viva voce* (a non-musician at an orchestral rehearsal, hearing the notes always referred to by their letter names, might well assume that all music was notated in letters). Letter and number notations offer the advantage that we are all trained to form and distinguish the symbols, so that we are well equipped to handle them. They also give us a means of distinguishing separately the degrees of a scale; a property that has been made use of in many teaching notations, and extended in solfa notation to form a system that relates every note to its position in the diatonic scale (see chapter 13).

41

Other lines of approach

If we take 'notation' in the broadest sense, to include all the ways in which directives may be issued, we should mention several other possible forms of communication.

1) *Gesture*

Many systems, from the Byzantine cantillation notations already mentioned (p. 8) to the solfeggio notations of our own day (p. 100) supplement the written script with an organized system of hand-gestures. The gestures of the conductor are also a form of supplementary notation. They generally (but not invariably) convey information of a sort, though too unsystematically to be classified as terms of a symbolic language. There is, however, no reason why a systematic language should not emerge. Boulez, we are told, 'has developed an elaborate, highly efficient system without baton, involving a direct translation of the music into arm, hand, and finger movements – a system which bears a particularly close relation to rhythm and attack, but in which every gesture, beside being functional, is particularly apt for the specific sound desired ... the complete independence of the two hands is fundamental'.[21]

2) *Sound-signals*

The drum-words of Indian music form a systematic vocal notation, the words and phrases 'representing a spoken and memorised system of fixed symbols which denote the various types and sequences of sounds to be performed'.[1] The use of sound signals is, clearly, inappropriate in most Western playing-situations; but this is overcome when a more sophisticated form of sound signal is used – the electronic bleeper, for use in music of high rhythmic complexity, by means of which signals can be fed to individual players through earphones. Use of this device opens the way to an exact co-ordination of parts in circumstances where rhythmic connections cannot be perceived by the players, since the whole sequence can be mathematically programmed in advance.[22]

3) *Light-signals*

Not often used, except for the co-ordination of far-flung groups of performers behind the scenes at the opera house. But Xenakis, in his *Strategie*, introduces a sort of scaffold hung with winking coloured lights from which the players take their cues.

4) *Direction by touch*

Used in Braille notations for the blind. The upper four of the six embossed dots of the standard system are used to specify the note, the lower two the time value. Braille music makes use of many abbreviations and deliberate abridgement to reduce the labour of reading note-by-note and to help blind readers to memorize easily. For keyboard music, the 'hand over hand' system is in general use; left and right hands are notated separately, as in conventional notation, and the player can learn the music by reading with one hand, and performing with the other.

5) *Words*

Lastly, one should mention the most obvious sort of symbolic direction of all – that written out in words. In the *Refined Orchid Book on Lute-playing*, an early Chinese instruction book, we find: 'put the middle finger about half an inch on the tenth *hui* and produce the *shang* tone. The second and middle jointly handle *kung* and *shang*. Hide the middle finger, and afterwards press it on the thirteenth *hui* in the form of a hook . . .'[1] Here, the Chinese writer anticipates the method of the avant-gardist Kagel, who, in his *Sonant*, instructs his bass player: 'You may begin, the guitarist has given the signal. Would you play two pizzicati molto vibrato on the Vth string at an interval of a minor ninth . . .?'; while Stockhausen, after working through many stages of notational evolution, was, in 1970, looking forward to a time when the score would consist of a few lines of inspirational text, to which players (possibly helped by teaching tapes to indicate general types of treatment or ensemble) would learn to respond intuitively.[23]

Solutions to problems on p. 39

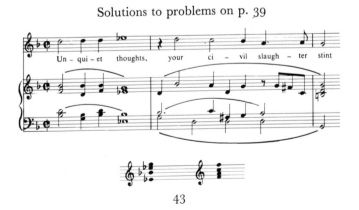

8 *Pitch*

The development of modern pitch notation from neume notation to stave has been such a devious process that any quick résumé is bound to misrepresent historical facts. In place of a historical précis, I give a model of the main stages of the process, to illustrate the significant gains and losses considered from the modern user's viewpoint.

1) Take three intonations of the word 'yes' and give an approximate indication of each by an appropriate accent sign:

Yes . . .   (considering, doubtful)

Yes.   (curt, businesslike)

Yes?   (question)

(The signs, like medieval neumes, can be used to distinguish three familiar alternatives – they suggest the shape of the word-tune, but their main function is to recall a familiar pattern)

2) A fixed line can be added to represent fundamental speaking tone:

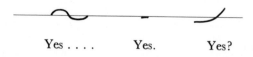

Yes . . . .   Yes.   Yes?

(corresponding to the first line added to neume notation – to indicate the home-tone, not a specific pitch)

44

3) Other lines can be added to define intervals in common use:

Yes . . . .   Yes.   Yes?

(corresponding to the gradual addition of the lines of the stave, to form, together with the spaces, a map of the diatonic scale)

4) On the analogy of alphabet writing, and on the single pitch signs, as at (b) below, each sign can be segmented. The sound continuum is divided up into distinct pitch levels:

Yes . . . . .   Yes   Yes?

(corresponding, in music, to the degrees of the diatonic scale)

5) The tune can be separated from the word. Pitch can be fixed to any degree of precision. (In normal use, we take c,d,e,f,g . . . to mean 'the sounds practising musicians accept as c,d,e,f,g . . . . '.):

6) We can return to the first notation, and convert it into a precise time-pitch graph, representing the sound as pitch-continuum, after the manner of today's proportionate notations:

Seconds   0 ——— ½ ——— 1 ——— 1½ — 2 ——— 2½

7) At (4), we have gained the power to specify many types of melodic pattern, but at the price of limiting our idea of 'melody' to 'that which can be notated by a series of

45

fixed pitches'. But we can still produce approximations to subtly inflected pronunciations:

Yes . . . .

In this example conventional time notation has at last appeared. In discussing the principles of staff notation, time and pitch notation are so closely interlocked that they must be taken in conjunction.

Principles of use

A) One sound – one symbol
B) One pitch – one level
C) Exact time-relationships shown in note-heads, stems, flags
D) Time-order: always left to right

Two characteristics set staff notation apart from all other notations, musical and non-musical, in common use.

1) In setting up the two axes on which pitch and time relationships are shown, the notation gives a direct graphical representation of the leading characteristics of the music. A split-second glance at a sheet of music evokes an overall impression, and forewarns the reader of the type of problem ahead of him.

2) A minimal range of symbols is used, the interpretation being fixed by context. There are two basic symbols, modifiable by the addition of tails, flags, sharps, flats, dots, etc. This limitation in number is an advantage to the writer, who has to learn to form them, and still more to the reader. We need to look less far into a musical script than a word script: if a wide range of symbols had to be individually identified and discriminated, we could never read so quickly.

The equally-gapped stave gives a fair enough picture of musical movement as it appears to us before we begin to analyse our experience. We sing our first tunes with no appreciation of large or small intervals, so that the regular spacing (like that of the white notes of the piano) seems to confirm our instinctive feeling that all intervals can be regarded as equal. There is a sort of truth in a notation that tells you only how many steps to take, and in which direction. The stave is not a scale map, but a diagram that establishes pitch order. It is no more misleading than those railway diagram-maps that represent distance between stations as equal; their function is simply to put the stations in order, so that the traveller knows where to get on or off. The advantage of this impartiality as to interval sizes is that a standardized stave can serve many purposes; if we had to indicate scale structure graphically, we would need a variably-gapped stave for every clef and key-change.

Changes of clef and key: chromatic notes

The practical result of a clef or key-change is to vary the tone-semitone order as it appears on the stave.

We see:

We deduce:

These adjustments introduce no contradiction or graphical complication into the system, the basic principles *one note – one level*, and *one tone – one symbol*, standing unaffected. It is when non-diatonic tones are introduced that we feel the disadvantages of a system that only provides for seven stations on the octave journey.

Because there are only seven niches, notes must share levels, upsetting the first basic principle, so that we can no longer rely on the visual guide to lead us to the right action:

A) Different notes on same level
B) Same note on different levels
C) Lower note on higher level

Because notes have to share levels, one must be distinguished by a double symbol, at the cost of increased labour for writer, and increased strain for reader, who must read further *into* the individual symbols to interpret them; the situation is further complicated by the need for cancelling accidentals:

Hindemith: Ludus Tonalis

Various bizarre alternatives have been suggested to meet these difficulties:[24]

1) Increasing the number of niches so that one can be allotted to each note:

2) Avoiding double symbols by using new symbols for non-diatonic tones:

3) Refining the spacing, while retaining the stave:

In modern proportional notations, where time is graphically measured solely by lateral displacement, whiteness and blackness can be used as pitch-indicators; thus Pousseur writes uninflected notes *black*, flattened notes *white*.

48

4) In Klavarscribo, a piano-orientated notation, unevenly
   spaced solid and dotted lines represent the black notes of
   the keyboard, while black and white notes are distinguished
   graphically. The notation is read vertically from top to
   bottom.

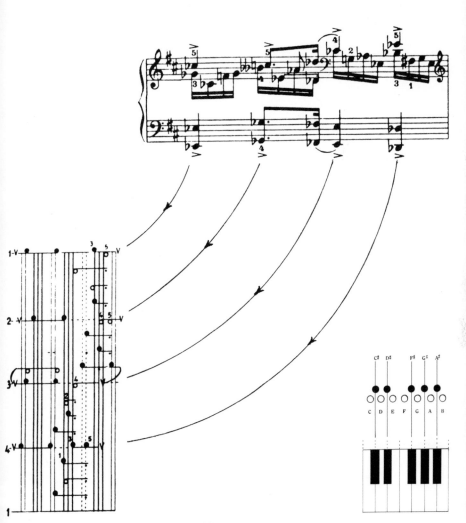

49

5) In Equitone, alternate notes appear black or white; the stave is replaced by two lines an octave apart, with five intermediate positions as shown, to cover the chromatic scale:

Less radically, Stockhausen has notated works in which all accidentals are written as sharps, considerably reducing the number of possible alternatives to be discriminated. The chief obstacle to the acceptance of any notational reform lies, of course, in the established habits of users, who have spent so much energy and time in learning to use the conventional language. There is another serious objection where a system that abolishes the flat-sharp distinction is used for diatonically-based music – that the sense of the music depends so often on the spelling. 'A note *must* be written as a sharp if it is felt that way, or a flat if it is to be understood as such, even if there is no difference between them on a tempered instrument'.[25] Even when the links with diatonicism have weakened, accidentals may still imply a sense of melodic direction:

Bartók: Mikrokosmos VI, no. 140

Limitations

By using both lines and spaces to represent tones, and by ignoring non-diatonic tones, the stave gains over its predecessors in compactness. With the addition of two ledger lines we can notate up to two octaves – a fair working range. Note the diffuseness of the more expansive system shown on page 48. Any increase in the number of stave lines is bound to increase the difficulty of identifying a note quickly from its position on the stave. It is inevitable that for wider-ranging instruments we have either to pile up unreadable skyscrapers of ledger lines or else to endure the graphical hiccups caused by changes of clef, or octave signs:

Beethoven: Piano Sonata op. 111

In practice, experienced players are little troubled by octave signs, which they find no more disconcerting than the jumps in word-reading from the end of one line to the beginning of the next. Ledger line tolerance is largely a matter of use. Flautists and violinists, who accept ledger lines as an occupational hazard, may even rewrite their parts so that a passage such as:

reads as

The stave reflects in its structure the medieval concept of a music in which the third is the smallest regular harmonic interval, with the second as an occasional and irregular intruder. Hence the awkward figuration which upsets the vertical alignment principle for simultaneously-sounding tones, and so often causes the note to be separated from its accidental by so wide an interval:

Ives:
Concord Sonata

The stave, because of its compactness, so advantageous in many ways, cannot cope with many notes crowded closely together; either they have to sprout from their stalks like grapes:

51

Bartók:
Mikrokosmos 133

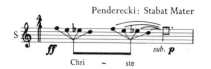

Penderecki: Stabat Mater

or the composer has to resort to 'all-in' devices such as the note-cluster signs, invented by Henry Cowell, and much used by Penderecki:

The symbols: should be played

With a sharp: =

With a natural: =

Keys to be pressed down silently:

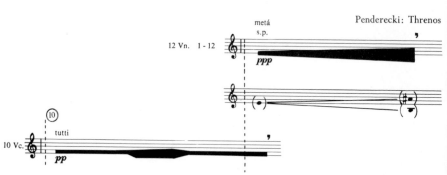

Penderecki: Threnos

One of the main reading difficulties has always been the use of unfamiliar clefs or transpositions. Today, the number of clefs in use has been greatly reduced (treble and bass alone serve most performers and most purposes), while the introduction of valved brass instruments, and the more versatile fingering systems of woodwind, has been followed by a reduction in the number of transpositions which the score-reader needs to interpret:

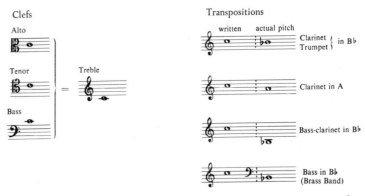

Clefs

Transpositions

Transposed parts appear in the 'natural' keys of instruments for the convenience of performers. In many recent scores (including Prokofiev's and Webern's) they are, however, written at actual pitch, in recognition of the truth that scores are no longer assemblages of parts, but accounts of the music designed to be read, not acted on. Logically, there is no reason why clefs should not also be standardized in the interests of the score-reader – alto and tenor could well be eliminated from the study-score.

One interesting move towards standardization has occurred in brass band scores, in which all instruments, down to the deepest basses, are notated in the treble clef, so that the tone-semitone stave pattern is identical in all cases. This practice probably stems from the versatility of brass band players, who often play several instruments, yet need only learn to read from a single clef; also, perhaps, from the fact that conductors of brass bands are themselves performers, and so prefer performer-orientated notations, while piano-conductor scores supply in this case the needs of the pianist score-reader.

Artificial harmonics on stringed instruments are normally notated according to fingerboard positions rather than the normal pitch-representation (though variations occur):

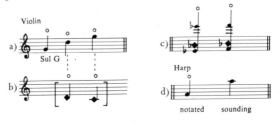

a) First, second, and third natural harmonics on violin G string notated at actual pitch
b) Alternative notation by finger-position
c) Artificial harmonics, showing { (above) actual pitch
                                     { (middle) note touched
                                     { (bottom) note stopped
   (The actual-pitch note is sometimes omitted)
d) Harp harmonic: sounds an octave up
Here too, notation follows the convenience of the player rather than that of the score-reader. Notice that string and harp natural harmonics are notated on different principles.

Developments

(Solo violin)   Berg: Chamber Concerto

[z = zwischentone]

a)   b)   c)

   Quarter tones are already intermittently in use, and the above example shows some of the notations adopted to symbolize the new tones. The most interesting developments in pitch notation, however, are not those which result in the establishment of new fixed intervals within the old system, but those which suggest a growing discrepancy between the needs of the users and the apparatus available. The discrepancy grows from the unstated assumption, implicit in the notational set-up, that the *pitch* of a note lies at the heart of the musical complex, and that we think music primarily in terms of pitch-relations. Yet as early as the 1920s, works were being written in which the precise pitch of any note had less importance than dynamic balance, timbre contrasts, or newly conceived patterns of density and spareness. In listening to works by Milhaud, Hindemith, or Schoenberg, it is often easy to feel that (whatever the claims made by composers themselves) it is becoming increasingly hard to receive the musical message in terms of harmonic relationships. Can you, for instance, say off-hand which of the following viola parts is the correct one (solution at end of chapter)?

The discomfort of the situation derives in part from the notational system itself, which binds the composer to certain patterns
of thinking and compels him to issue orders in the form of 'this-or-
that-level' for each separate step forward, when he may have
already switched attention to aspects of musical experience that
are only remotely connected with note-by-note pitch relationships.

These are the circumstances under which composers have
begun to look for ways to free themselves from the discipline
imposed by the stave; sometimes by taking new freedoms within
the system, sometimes by doing away with the system altogether:

Earle Brown: Available forms II

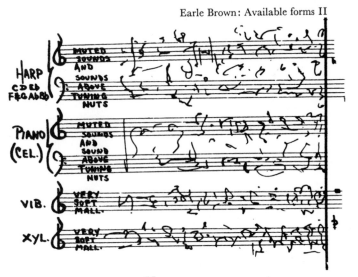

55

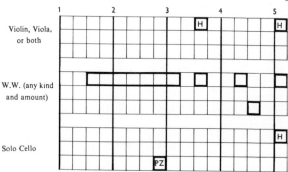

Squares horizontally represent a time-unit of M.M.72. 'Vertically, each of the three squares represents a general pitch level: low, medium, and high. Each instrument comes in when its part has a blocked-in square, but once it has entered, the tone or tones must remain until the blocked-in square ends. Sometimes the composer indicates by an H that he wishes harmony, or by Pz that a pizzicato tone would be appreciated.'[26]

Lukas Foss: Echoi

2) Bend quarter-tone down
3) Bell over piano for extra resonance
4) Any notes on way up or down
5) Pitchless sounds

(Solution to problem on p. 55: the middle viola line is correct.)

9 Time

Today, we all work with a single standardized time notation system, by means of which each individual note can be assigned a definite length and a precise place in the time sequence. Medieval time notation is confusing to today's interpreters, both because of the many different systems used, and because of the different attitudes of users. Medieval notators do not seem to have felt the need of a mathematically precise, note-by-note, time specification. 'In the thirteenth century the group we call meter or foot was a whole with precedence over the individual note. It presented a certain arrangement of long and short syllables, but not of definite time values. It was up to (the musician) to allot unmistakable values to these members without ever forgetting they were longs and breves, whether he gave them one, two, or three units – even when a breve happened to become as long as an actual *lunga*.'[27] So, too, the notation of a dance in duple time did not commit the player to perform it only in duple time – the piece could be played in ternary rhythm without losing its identity. Nor was the ordering of long and short notes necessarily regarded as a basic characteristic of music. A treatise of 1279, explaining the use of the *ligatura binarii*, declares that 'its parts must be played unequally, as is the truth. At the same time, however, one may be doubtful about their order . . . . .'[28] Symbols could, too, be used in different senses in different contexts: 'today, a breve always contains four minims; in the fourteenth century it might contain anything from four to twenty-four, according to the nationality of the man who wrote it down on paper and the context in which it occurs.'[6] Signs could change meaning according to their place in relation to one another – so, in the thirteenth century, three consecutive breves might each stand for a note of different duration. It was the spread of polyphony in the fourteenth and fifteenth centuries that made necessary both the strict, note-by-note synchronization of parts and the unambiguous time notation in which the more stringent timetable could be written out. The existence of the theoretical timetable does not, of course, guarantee that notes (or trains) run strictly to time. The idea of limited flexibility within the rhythmic group persists, and established performing conventions may run counter to the explicit sense of the notations, as in eighteenth-century *notes inégales* and double-dotting conventions, in the use of ♩. ♩ in certain contexts for  (see p. 34), and, in our own day, in the idiomatic bending of the even three-note waltz rhythm by Viennese bands, and the conventional jazzing-up of written rhythms by dance band players. But the principles of unambiguous time notation are understood and accepted by all, and have remained unchanged since the sixteenth century.

Principles of use

The same principle lies behind word-writing and music-writing; in each case, the symbols for individual sounds are arranged on a time-chart, reading from left to right. The arrangement gives the order in time, but no more. In word-writing, the rate at which symbols succeed one another is left to the discretion of the reader: in music, we look to the noteheads themselves to discover the duration of each tone. The extent of lateral displacement is, theoretically, of no significance: in practice, beats of equal length tend (other things being equal) to fill roughly equal amounts of lateral space. We therefore come to rely on the amount of space taken as a guide to the length of tones, and may be confused in irregular situations – when, for instance, the need to overlay words of varying length distorts the normal spacing pattern.

The 'order' principle implies that simultaneous sound events appear in vertical alignment. But up to the beginning of the nineteenth century, a great deal of latitude was acceptable in the alignment of parts. In earlier days, the score was never designed to be taken in as a coherent whole, and even when parts were designed for simultaneous performance by one player, as in keyboard music, little attempt was made at strict alignment. In performing the Handel example shown here, we could probably allow for the inconsistencies in layout:

Handel: Organ Concerto No. 4

the difficulties of sightreading the Parthenia score (below) would, for the modern player at least, probably be insuperable.

Parthenia (the first music to be engraved in England; note the six-line stave)

Today, layout of simultaneous parts is arranged strictly according to the rule of vertical alignment. Where irregular groups appear in combination, we may find a reversal of the earlier position, in that the notation is much more precise than any likely realization in sound.

Time relationships; dots and ties; irregular groups
Conventional notation allows for proportional time relationships in simple duple form only, as shown by the familiar chart:

The most awkward limitation of the system is that there is no provision for third-ing; we are perpetually in the position of the mother of three who can only buy sponge cakes in packets of two, four, or eight, and is therefore always short, or left with a residue. Hence the complexities of compound time notation,* so confusing

---

* Arthur Jacobs, as well as many others, has objected to the 'unnecessary, unfunctional verbalising' in distinguishing 'compound' and 'simple' time.[29] The words (and the complexity) belong wholly to the notational situation, and have no foundation in sound. It is still simpler, if less logical, to distinguish ⅝ from ¾ by calling it 'compound' instead of defining it as 'six eighth-notes grouped as three plus three'.

to the beginner:

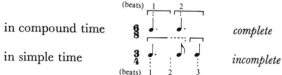

And to notate the musically commonplace nine-beat bar, we have to glue together a large one-and-a-half and a small one-and-a-half, thus:

A further cause of confusion lies in the doubt as to whether a dotted crotchet represents a complete or incomplete metrical unit:

The fusing together of noteheads by use of the tie, made necessary where lengths cannot be expressed as simple multiples of unit-values, or when a note is held over a barline, is another makeshift solution, producing complexities in the notation which have no equivalent in sound. The appearance of noteheads that have no separate sound-identity is a cause of confusion to the learner, who has to be gradually persuaded *not* to sound separately the second of two tied notes; while the aggressive symbolization of unheard beats increases his difficulty in thinking across the barline. Sixteenth century dotted notation here gives a truer picture of the 'feel' of prolongation:

Use of multiple ties can make for extreme notational complexity in simple situations:

Brahms: Intermezzo op. 119, no. I

But common-sense solutions can be often found for such problems:

Messiaen: Chronochromie

The notation of irregular groups by means of the familiar figure under a square bracket means that crotchet and minim may be called upon to serve in different capacities. It often happens that the same symbol appears in rapid succession in a series of roles, or simultaneously in several parts, bearing a different meaning at each appearance.each appeance. In the following example, each ringed crotchet has a different duration:

Britten: Songs and Proverbs of William Blake op. 74

The situation shown above is self-explanatory. But where fluctuating time signatures are in use, or the unit of subdivision is not explicitly stated, or where irregular groups appear across barlines, or *within* other irregular groups, it may be a long and difficult task to discover the intended meaning – and even then the instruction still has to be acted on:

Ives: 3 places in New England

Stravinsky: Abraham and Isaac

In Ex. (b): Bar 1: *Think* three quavers and *play* five against them. Bar 2: *Think* five semiquavers and *play* three quavers against them. The (thought) beat provides the unheard constant.

Stockhausen: Klavierstück I

In Ex. (c):

1) *Think* a basic 5-crotchet beat.
2) *Think* eleven quavers in the time of the 10 first thought of.
3) *Play* six quavers in this new tempo.
4) Against the five quavers you have left, which you are already *thinking* against the original (unheard) 5-crotchet beat, *think* 7 quavers . . . and so on.

The combination of irregular groups creates great difficulties for performers; it is certainly easier to notate eleven against ten than to perform it (though even notating it is not so very simple; Gardner Read gives up 24 pages of his *Notation* to graphs that show exactly how different irregular groups should be aligned). Traditionally trained performers, who expect to perform music as it is written, may be perturbed by the apparently meaningless precision of notations, as a conversation between Yfrah Neaman and Howard Ferguson bears out:[30]

Y.N. Talking of rhythms: I've often wondered whether composers who write, say, seventeen notes against eleven really expect the result to be mathematically correct, or do they only expect an approximation?

H.F. I haven't an idea what they expect; but I know that, short of electro-mechanical reproduction, they will generally get an approximation.

Barlines

The barline has three functions: to indicate metre, to point up irregular stresses, and to serve as a reference point. Each of these uses will be considered in turn.

1) *Metre*

When regular barlines outline the regular metre, they may or may not coincide with the pattern of surface stresses which we actually hear. In a conventional march, metrical divisions and stress points will coincide, so that the first beat receives a heavier stress, the third a lighter, as prescribed by the rudiments books:

Schubert: Marches Héroiques op. 5

Where a secondary metre is run against the primary metre, this will appear as a syncopation running against the sense of the barline:

J. Strauss: Voices of Spring op. 410

The underlying metre, felt but never heard, may be played off in rhythmic counterpoint against less regular patterns of stress and rhythm set up by word-accentuation or varying types of motive-development:

Morley

Fire   and   light – ning from Heav'n fall, Fire and light – ning from Heav'n fall,

The beginners (and others) who seem to assume that every barline is to be marked with a bump are most often those who have been over-exposed to tunes of the first type, and imagine that, because they have so far been called on to place a stress at each barline, the barline is to be read as a stress-directive wherever it occurs.

2) *Stress*

When metrical regularity is non-existent, the barline, released from metrical duties, can be used to indicate stress alone:

169   Stravinsky: Rite of Spring

The point at which a metre becomes so irregular as to be imperceptible is hard to locate; in the example above, we might say that the notation directs us to *feel* the stresses rather than to emphasize each bar with an accent. It is at least safe to say that the barline is used to show the rhythmic patterning, actual or imagined, and that this will in some circumstances call for an active interpretation in the form of accentuation.

3) *Reference*
The barline may serve as reference point only, with no implication of rhythm or stress. So, in some Mozart adagios, bar-divisions may be twice as long as the metrical unit, so that a leading theme may arrive back indifferently at the beginning of a bar, or halfway through a bar. Or else no metre at all may be perceptible, as in

Schoenberg: Pierrot Lunaire (Der Kranke Mond)

Sehr langsam ♩ = 96 - 100

In all conducted music, the barline becomes the vital point of verbal *and visual* reference. It is the place where (the player hopes) the conductor's stick will come *down*. The less comprehensible the music, the greater the importance of this visual reference.

Polyrhythms
Till the end of the nineteenth century, the convention was generally accepted that the metre of a movement was fixed once for all, in the first bar, and the subsequent developments took place within the established metrical framework:
a) Borrowed beats must be repaid:

Wagner: Meistersinger

b) Temporary or 'irregular' rhythms must be fitted into one of the established measures:

Today, we are able both to conceive and to notate irregular rhythms and metres without restriction:

a) Beats may be freely added or subtracted:

Stravinsky: Octet

b) Temporary or irregular rhythms may be defined in irregular barring:

Copland: Nonet

One effect of this new freedom is to introduce an element of wider choice into time notation – we can choose which particular sense we wish to make of the music. When we notate polyrhythms, problems of choice are often critical. We can *either* give each rhythm its appropriate notation, in which case the barline no longer serves as common reference point; *or* choose a uniform barlength for all parts, notating, where necessary, across the barline – in which case only one of the rhythms will be visually represented in the notation. In unconducted ensembles, the first method may be used; notice, however, that in the example below, Bartók has notated the ¾ independently for viola, while leaving the cello imitation in ²/₄ (perhaps baulking at the idea of three simultaneous time signatures):

Bartók: 3rd Quartet

In conducted music, the barline must be kept as a point of visual reference common to all. Copland bows to necessity by notating a $(\frac{5}{8} + \frac{3}{8})$ in $\frac{3}{8}$:

(for the conductor)   Copland : Dance Symphony

(for the player)

Even with the help of beaming, the meaning is obscured for the player. Copland compromises by adding a supplementary stave, so that the conductor, at least, may be made aware of the true sense of the passage.

When a choice arises, as in the examples above, composers tend to prefer the notation that exposes the *sense* of the music, players that which keeps the common reference points (in poly-rhythms), or avoids ever-changing time signatures. The solution does not, of course, depend only on the convenience of the player; there is a counterpoint between a (felt) visual rhythm and a mani-fest sound rhythm which alters the whole sense of the above example for the reader, when the music is read from the lower version. Schumann introduces a counterpoint between the (heard) duple rhythm and the (imagined) three beats of the basic rhythm in the finale of his piano concerto. Here, the conductor's baton may supply the clue for the audience, yet in everyday contexts it is quite easy for the player or listener to supply an unheard rhythm. The following example, from an elementary recorder book, con-sists of a single melodic line. The pattern is so familiar that any player or listener can be expected to follow the sense, written and sounding:

Arditi: Il Bacio

Some rhythmically complex passages can be thought of as having a meaning that lies halfway between written and sounding notes. In the examples below, excitement and tension are en-hanced by the way in which notes dodge the barline. The lower version of Ex. (c) below, given in regular barlengths, would have a different feel to it for player or score-reader, though the sounds notated are identical. To determine the precise difference of effect on the non-literate listener is, of course, quite impossible. Here

66

again, as in the Schumann concerto, the visual impact of the conductor's beat must be thought of as helping to establish the true rhythmic pattern for the listener-viewer.

Stravinsky: Rite of Spring

Time signatures

Conventional time signatures, in which the upper figure stands for the number of beats and the lower figure stands for the pulse unit, are adequate in situations where bars are built up with identical time-units, and where metres keep to simple multiple relationships. Any recurring metre can be easily notated by an extension of the system that allows for subdivisions within the bar or combinations of alternating patterns such as:

a) $\frac{4\frac{1}{2}}{4}$ or $\frac{4}{4} + \frac{1}{8}$ or $\frac{8+1}{8} =$

b) $\frac{3+2+3}{8}$ or $\frac{3}{8}\frac{2}{8}\frac{3}{8} =$

Note that there is a certain amount of choice available, and that there is slight but perceptible difference in the implication of stress between the various versions. Holst's *Perfect Fool* music in $\frac{7}{8}$ would show the seams between rhythmic units more clearly if notated as $\frac{4+3}{8}$, and more clearly again as $\frac{4}{8}\frac{3}{8}$:

Holst: The Perfect Fool

67

Constant use of irregular metres and rhythms results in music full of varying and often unfamiliar time signatures. The haphazard way in which we notate signatures becomes a real inconvenience when we have to read, at speed, sequences such as: $\frac{5}{16}$ $\frac{2}{8}$ $\frac{3}{16}$ $\frac{5}{16}$ $\frac{2}{8}$ (from Stravinsky's *Abraham and Isaac*) where the true bar-proportions would be represented by the sequences 5 4 3 5 4.

Various reformed notations are intermittently in use. In time-signatures, the lower figure may be replaced by the appropriate note $\frac{3}{}$ (clear, but going against the principle that notes are for playing). Recognizing the fact that the barline may constitute a psychological barrier to the free flow of music, some composers lift the line clear of the stave (a), or revert to the partial barlines found in medieval music, whose only function is to serve as point of reference (b):

a)   Stravinsky   b)   Berio

Tempo

Some speak of having recourse to the Motion of a lively pulse for the Measure of *Crotchets*, or to the little Minutes of a steddy going Watch for Quavers. . . .
                                                              (Christopher Simpson, 1665)[31]

How uncertain must be the value of mathematics in music.

(Richard Wagner, on deciding to discontinue the use of metronome markings in his music)[32]

Practical musicians have, during long periods of musical history, been content to find the right tempo by intuition rather than by measurement – perhaps sensing that the choice of a 'right' tempo is closely bound up with the acoustics of the playing space, the timbre of the particular instruments involved, and the articulation habits of players. In earlier ages, appropriate tempo was implied by the note forms, the time signatures, by the title of the piece (each traditional dance or song carrying its own implication of tempo), by mood indication or the brief word directives still in use. The invention of the metronome, at the end of the eighteenth century, introduced a tempo notation that was too precise for most users and most occasions; we still find that, in performance, metronome markings are rarely observed with anything like the devotion accorded to almost any other type of composers' markings. New types of tempo control, and new signs, have been evolved over the last few decades. Proportional notations are often divided into time sections measured in round seconds – from the four-second 'bars' of Bedford's *White and Radiant Legend* to the thirty-second divisions of Cage's *Atlas Eclipticalis*. Though these divisions are included ostensibly for reference purposes, musical events still have a way of grouping themselves within divisions – a hangover, perhaps, from times when the bar still represented the structural unit. Another way of establishing tempo is to give the total time to be taken for the piece. The '58 sec.' at the end of a Bartók piano piece may, perhaps, be read as description rather than direction – the time that a typical performance might take (or again, it might be included to help copyright calculations). Cage's picturesquely titled *27'10.554" for a percussionist* seems to go beyond the range of human judgement and should perhaps be entered up as a 'paradoxical' notation.* Another form of tempo notation, used by Stockhausen in his first four piano pieces, is to mark the smallest note values to be played 'as fast as possible' and relate all other speeds to this fastest speed. At the other end of the scale, long notes may be marked to be held to extinction – in which case tempo is very practically linked to the special circumstance prevailing at performance.

One by-product of the introduction of the metronome, and of clock-measured tempi, has been to relieve the notes themselves of the duty of implying any tempo at all. In medieval music, it is possible to generalize, even if tentatively, about the tempo implications of breves and semibreves: semibreve = 80 has been suggested as the norm round about 1350. We can also trace the evolutionary process in which note values became steadily devalued, till by the end of the eighteenth century the semibreve had become the longest note in common use, while with new subdivisions of lesser units, semiquavers and demisemiquavers had taken over at the quick end of the tempo scale. This process we can now see to have ended. With unambiguous tempo notation we can arbitrarily fix the length of any note, so that the reason for choosing any type of note as the basic unit will be found in aesthetic or psychological preferences – or in a belief that certain formations will make for easier reading.

Recent developments
Conventional notation has long been concerned with the exact

* See p. 141.

synchronization of musical movement. The strict prohibitions of traditional harmony and counterpoint have made it essential that music shall move to a timetable, notes arriving and departing punctually so as to avoid all chance collisions. In new, permissive harmonic situations, parts may be allowed to run free, the principal question being, where, when, and how to bring them together again? The new situation has evoked some wordy instructions (Boulez takes forty-eight words to explain the sign ⌐‾‾¬ which directs notes to be played in free tempo within a held pause), and one sign at least which is of real value—Britten's 'curlew'. This sign (above the word 'God') indicates that the singer must listen and wait till the pianist has reached the next barline:

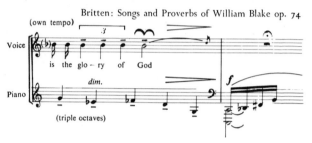

Britten: Songs and Proverbs of William Blake op. 74

Proportionate notation

The principle underlying proportionate notation is that durations should be exactly represented on the horizontal time axis. The old system of time notation may be retained, but with each note placed strictly in position on the time graph, so that the player is given what is in effect a double time notation.

Lumsdaine: Kelly Ground

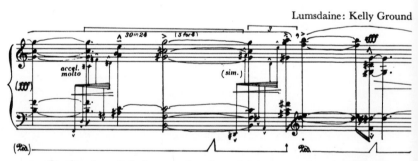

Or the time-defining noteheads and beams can be abandoned altogether. There are three types of pure proportionate notation in general use:

a) The tone may be shown by a continuous line

b) The starting-point may be shown by a notehead, followed by a continuous line

c) The length of the tone may be shown by a beam, which shows duration independently of pitch.

The double notation of Lumsdaine's *Kelly Ground* seems to offer a very small gain in exchange for a great amount of labour for engraver or copyist, and eliminates none of the inconsistencies of conventional time notation. The advantages of a fully proportionate notation are great:

1) The direct graphical approach gives an immediate analogue for duration of tones.
2) The continuity of graphical line gives a better picture of the legato of successive tones than the separated symbols of conventional notation.
3) Many of the inconsistencies of conventional notation can be bypassed; dotted notes and ties vanish, accelerandi and rallentandi can be precisely notated (see the next section for the problems involved).
4) Noteheads and beams are freed from time-defining duties, and can be used for other purposes.*
5) Notation of silence (rests) becomes unnecessary.

The disadvantages of proportionate notation are also great. A proportionate notation can never help us to perceive the beat structure fundamental to traditionally structured music. As Kurt Stone has said, 'Human beings simply do not seem to possess a space perception equal in acuity to their pulse perception: if they are not given something they can count, they will not be able to play "in time".'[33] Proportionate notations can be most successfully used where there is a wish to escape from the conventional

---

* White and black can be used to indicate flattening and sharpening (see p. 49), legato and staccato, soft and loud. Beams can be used explicitly and solely to show articulation patterns, or accelerando and ritenuto (see p. 73).

time-framework into a world where there is no suggestion of background pulse. Compromises can, however, be effected; Berio successfully combines proportionate and conventional notations, using them for non-metrical and metrical sections within a single work.

The difficulty of producing an accurate proportionate score, in which every length must be precisely measured, is another serious drawback. It is no accident that notations rely so completely on the quickly-formed dot and dash and the prefabricated stave. When we come to list the desired attributes of a practical notation, *quick-to-write* comes almost as high on the list as *easy-to-read*.

Accelerando and rallentando

Contemporary composers have shown interest in the controlling of processes of accelerando and rallentando. These may be written into the note-values to obtain a 'tempo glissando' in one part while others continue in strict tempo. In the following example, the figures give note-values in crotchets and the dotted line indicates the extent of the accelerando. The complexities of thus running against the grain of the notation are formidable, and we may doubt if the end-result will ever match the nicety of the directive. This is a case where use of proportionate notation would simplify the notational situation without any loss in accuracy of statement:

Elliot Carter: 2nd Quartet

a) extent of accelerando
b) length of individual notes in crotchets

Where reformed notation has freed the beams of the notes for new duties, accelerando and rallentando may be elegantly built in:

Stockhausen: Klavierstück X

a)   accel.   rit.   very fast

b) Connolly: Obbligati II

(rit.)

mf ——— *f*

Arrows or sloping lines may be used, with or without metronome marks, for speeding and slowing:

(Graded inclinations)   Boulez: Pli selon pli

a) 1 o→   2 o↗   3 o↗   4 o↗   o = 144
                                          4 = 231

In Stockhausen's *Klavierstück VI* the highest line corresponds to the fastest tempo, the thick middle line to a tempo half as fast, the lowest line to a tempo half as fast as that. Between the extremes (1:4) the player should establish a tempo scale with 12 intervals that are perceived as equal.

10 *Dynamics and Timbre*

Dynamic balance

When we notate time and pitch, we are dealing with stable elements of musical sound. In notating dynamics, we move forward into a region where nothing is fixed. The values indicated by the signs *ff*, *f*, *p*, *pp*, etc. are not only relative but entirely dependent on context. Our judgement of loudness is affected by distance from the sound source; by the acoustic conditions of the moment; by pitch; and by the timbre of whatever instrument we happen to be listening to. Dynamic balance depends on so many varied and unpredictable features, that at every performance adjustments have to be made which cannot be allowed for in advance. The symbols themselves therefore talk in a general way. Not only do they present no more than an ordering of loudnesses; they must also allow for the fact that, in the course of a few bars, *p* or *f* may require widely different interpretations. To balance a chord between instruments, or to ensure that a single part stands out with just the right amount of prominence, loudnesses may have to be increased or diminished by many perceptible degrees.

Stokowski at one time measured loudnesses with a phonometer, on a scale reading from *pp* 40 phons to *fff* 95 phons. 'One would like to know', A. L. Lloyd has asked, 'how successfully this loudness-meter estimates the loudness of the notes of the bass instruments, as compared with that of an instrument of high pitch. For as we move to notes in the bass stave and below, that are lower and lower in pitch, the ear requires them to vibrate with increasing intensity before it accepts them as sounding equally loud.'[34] Did Stokowski site his phonometer in the most expensive seats in the hall, or where? (You can't be right for everybody: Furtwängler, told his *pp* was inaudible at the back, said 'it does not matter; they do not pay so much'.) And what would the phonometer have made of the Walton markings shown below?

The difficulty of specifying how sections of the orchestra are to balance against each other can be faced in different ways. Beethoven specifies over-all dynamic level, then leaves it to the men on the spot to make appropriate adjustments. Tchaikovsky, in reducing the brass marking by one degree, includes a warning to brass players not to overpower the rest of the orchestra. Walton, in a contrapuntal tutti, envisages a wide range of intensities – or

74

rather 'degrees of prominence' – since there can be no standard of comparison between, say, a high flute note *mp* and a double bass note *p*. All diversified markings of this type must be read as instructions to the conductor. Without guidance, the horn *pp* cannot know that the flute is marked *mp*, the bassoon *mf*, and it is only in the light of such knowledge that his own marking becomes meaningful.

Beethoven	Woodwind *ff*	*Walton*	Fl. *mp*
	Brass *ff*		Brass *ff*
	Strings *ff*		Ob. at top of cresc. from *pp*
			Bsns. *mf*
			Hns. *pp*
			Vn.I *mf*
			Vn.II *mp* espress.
			Va. no mark since *ppp*
Tchaikovsky	Woodwind *fff*		*poco cresc.*
	Brass *ff*		Celli *mf*
	Strings *fff*		D.b. *p*

   The amount of detail in dynamic marking varies according to the practical and aesthetic views of composers. Hindemith and (in later works) Stravinsky are sparing in their use of dynamics, as if in protest against the distracting emotional effect of continual dynamic fluctuation. In Cardew, dynamics may be rare for quite another reason: ' "Dynamics are free" does not mean that there are to be no dynamics, or one constant dynamic, but invites the player to ask himself "what dynamic(s) for this sound?" thus bringing himself into the position of having to take care of the sound, putting it in his charge, making him responsible.'[35] In Stockhausen and Boulez works, on the other hand, every note may carry its own dynamic:

Stockhausen: Kreuzspiel

This type of marking is more revolutionary than it looks; while we are brought up to a language of terraced pitch levels and time values, traditional vocal and instrumental performing styles imply an even flow of tone, and that each phrase should be considered as a dynamic entity. To perform such passages as the Stockhausen involves a break with long established tradition, as hard to accomplish as a break with normal accentuation patterns in speech.

How many dynamic degrees can usefully be distinguished? It is probably true that orchestras are today trained to play both louder and softer than at any previous time, so that an increasingly wide scale of dynamics can reasonably be employed to fit the situation. The twelve-level dynamic scale, from *pppp* to *ffff* used by some total serialists (by analogy with the twelve tones of the chromatic scale) is at least a practical possibility. Duo-Art player-pianos gave a range of fifteen variations of tone, and so of dynamic, which was enough to satisfy the many famous pianists who recorded for them – suggesting that the limit of discrimination lies somewhere round this point. This is not, of course, to say that these variations could be used in regular ascending order of intensity so as to make the order perceptible to listeners, since durations, timbres, and pitches all affect perception of loudness to an extent that makes direct comparison impossible. In practice we must also allow for the fact that performers allow themselves a great deal of licence in interpreting dynamics. Even in performances of classical music, distinctions between *p* and *pp*, *f* and *ff*, are constantly overlooked. Practical composers make some allowance for such attitudes: the *pppppp* in Tchaikovsky's Sixth Symphony should perhaps be read as an urgent plea for attention rather than as literal instruction – 'forget all other *pp*s if you must, but *on no account* overlook this one'.

Conventional dynamic signs suffer for their relatively late arrival on the notational scene by being separated from the note; they are also (except for the ⎯=⎯) non-graphical. Recent reforms have aimed to build dynamic into the system, and to represent it graphically. Stockhausen's original plan to notate his *Carré* by lines of twelve different thicknesses (representing loudnesses) wandering over a time-pitch graph, has an attractive simplicity about it but raised impossible problems for copyist and engraver. Other graphical devices are shown below. Note that once the dynamic is represented graphically, notation cannot be indeterminate: a note is one size and no other.

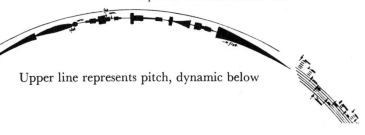

Kupkovic: Für Bassklarinette allein

Upper line represents pitch, dynamic below

Bartolozzi: New Sounds for Woodwind[36]

Dynamic indicated by thickening of beam

Cage: Changes

Numbers indicate dynamic levels

Stockhausen: Zyklus

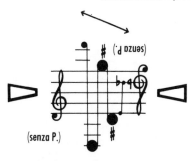

Arrow indicates ritenuto
Loudness shown by size of notehead

77

Notation of timbre

The story told by the ethnomusicologist Mantle Hood, of the old and blind Chinese musician who could identify any player at the first stroke of the great gong,[37] brings out the difference between a music in which timbre and mode of attack are of central importance, and one in which they are, comparatively, a matter of indifference. 'Meaning' in Western music is a matter of pitch, time, and, occasionally, of dynamics. Timbre, as far as it is notated at all, is relegated to the 'manner of performance' category. *What we play* (the notes) is separated from *how we play* (timbre, articulation, mode of attack). The notes themselves may be supposed to imply the right 'manner', just as the words of the playscript imply the inflection and accentuation for the actor.

Two limitations affect the development of timbre notations:

1) Timbre variation is only to a limited extent under the performer's control. The nature of the sound is limited in advance by physical make-up, instrument, embouchure, established methods of tone-production.

2) Timbre variations cannot be objectively described in terms meaningful to the performer.

The first limitation ensures that we already have a crude timbre notation available, which we use every time we choose or name an instrument or voice: in scoring a piece for oboe and violin rather than for trumpet and flute, we are selecting timbres. The second limitation explains the vagueness of timbre notations, and their indirect form. In calling for finer deviations, we can only refer to known models, or make metaphorical comparisons, or call for the actions needed to produce special types of sound.

A precise tone quality may be indicated by reference to a known model; thus, the quilisma of medieval neume notation implied a particular manner of performance known to all users. In like manner, we find in French opera scores a voice-quality defined by referring to a traditional type of singer; 'Trial', the high, reedy tenor used in Ravel's *L'enfant et les Sortilèges*, and 'Baritone-Martin', are named after the singers who first developed this type of sound. The markings 'flautando' in a violin part, 'cuivré' for brass, 'with white tone' for clarinet (that is, neutral) introduce a metaphorical element – the important thing is, of course, not that the comparison or metaphor should be a just one (flutes do not sound flautando; all brass instruments might be expected, of their nature, to play brassily) but that everyone should know what is expected of them. Where there is no common background of

78

traditional practice we may resort to extra-musical comparisons:
'Commonly used terms such as "tense", "relaxed", "pulsating",
"pinched-voiced", etc. are very general and, moreover, seem to
have meaning only to those already acquainted with different
singing styles. One is tempted to follow the example of a student
of South American Indians who stated that one singer, according
to his compatriots, sounded like a cow, and added, "He did".'
(Bruno Nettl)[38]

Many instrumental modifications of timbre involve physical or
mechanical adaptation, and in this case the timbre can be notated
as an action rather than a sound. Most of these directives are
written out – pizzicato, con sordino, sul tasto, vibrato, sul
ponticello, etc. It is strange that only a few of the less-used
directives have developed their own signs, such as snap-pizzicato
(Bartók): ⊖ and left hand pizzicato: +.

Avant-garde scores, however, are full of special signs for new
playing activities. New uses of prepared pianos, new methods of
colouring or splitting woodwind tones, as well as such marginally
musical activities as mouthpiece-blowing, key-tapping, and valve-
rattling have produced whole vocabularies of new symbols.
Although new timbres are produced as a result of these activities,
it is perhaps stretching a point to describe them as timbre notations, when the significance as often lies in the action itself:

(a) Special effects for woodwind:

Bartolozzi:
New Sounds for Woodwind

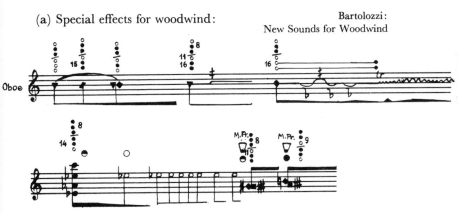

White noteheads indicate smorzato. Different shapes indicate
different tone colours and harmonic sounds. Beam thickness
indicates dynamic.

♯♭ quarter tones   ♯♯♭ threequarter tones

79

lun-a-tic who has been deft – ly warned

(arco)

(woodwind). Play on the removed reed or mouthpiece, *Glissando* by lip pressure

(woodwind). Rattle the fingers rapidly on the keys.

(b) Special effects for percussion (piano):

Kagel: Transicion II

𝕏 , 𝕏 indirect beating : one does not hit the string or body of the piano directly, but hits another stick which is placed upon it. (When playing with both hands : 𝕏 = with finger nails)

‖/ cluster (no gliss); inclination of the rectangle refers to position of stick on the strings

┃ cluster-glissando, simultaneously in both directions

(c) Special effects for strings:

Penderecki: First Quartet

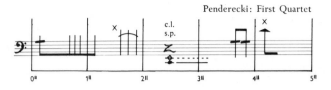

c.l.	col legno	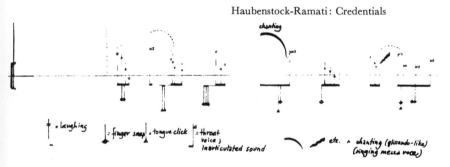	play between bridge and
s.p.	sul ponticello		tailpiece (on three strings)
x	legno battuto		
⋜	quite a rhythmic tremolo		percussive: play with bow
↑	high note		or fingernail on belly

(d) Special effects for voice:

Haubenstock-Ramati: Credentials

‡ = laughing   = finger snap = tongue click = throat voice; Inarticulated sound   etc. = chanting (glissando-like) (singing mezza voce)

11 *Articulation and Phrasing*

Staccato

Use of the staccato mark reintroduces ambiguity into time notation. Three reasons can be suggested why we should prefer to use
an indeterminate marking for shortening notes rather than a
combination of notes and rests:

1) In a resonant hall, we may start a note – but who is to say
   when it will end? The vagueness of the staccato mark is an
   admission of the fact that only the man on the spot is in a
   position to decide on the proper course of action.

2) Musical meaning is vested in the beginning, not the end,
   of a note. The extra labour of defining the exact moment of
   ending may be greater than the gain in musical significance
   warrants.

3) A rest may signify a break in the flow of the music, where
   a staccato mark leaves continuity unbroken. The message
   given may then be not 'a series of detached notes' but 'a
   continuous series of notes played in a detached manner' –
   a slight, but significant difference. Note the different impact of these two Beethoven extracts:

The staccato mark, normally used to indicate a shortening of
the end of a note, may indicate separation from the preceding
note:

Confusion is avoided in such contexts if (as Bartók suggests)
the dot is placed *within* the slur to show an interruption before the
last note; *outside* to show a shortening of the last note:

Accents

$$sf, \mathbf{v}(\mathbf{\Lambda}), >, \mathbf{v} \; (= \cdot + >)$$

The series given above represents (in approximate order of intensity) the accent signs available today. The element of choice is wide, the distinctions between grades of accent often doubtful. It is often hard to decide whether a composer meant anything at all by a variation of sign; even in such a carefully notated work as Stravinsky's *Rite of Spring*, it is difficult to be certain of the intention at all points. The mark $\mathbf{v}$, we may note, is never used for a lighter accent than the mark $\succ$, but the two are sometimes used as though interchangeable – as between rehearsal numbers 53 and 54, where half the wind have one mark, half the other. The $>$ mark alone is used if the first of two slurred notes is accented – does this, or does it not, imply a diminuendo? – and do we infer that the $\mathbf{v}$ mark is unsuitable because it carries a suggestion of shortening? The many *sf* marks seem generally to require a greater accentuation than $\succ$ marks; but at times the two are used in parallel contexts. the combined mark (accent + staccato) is often reinforced by a *sf*. How, if at all, is this to be distinguished in performance from the plain staccato dot +*sf*? Is a reinforced sign ($sf + \succ$) stronger than the single sign $\succ$, or purely precautionary? It would be pedantic to bother much about such points; but they indicate the wide difference between the languages of pitch and time, and the languages of dynamics and articulation. In the former, writers and readers expect to send and receive precise, unambiguous orders, and the language is adapted to specify an exact position and duration. In notation of dynamics and articulation, we choose signs because we *feel* them to be appropriate to the occasion, and interpret according to the spirit, rather than the letter.

Graphical and mechanical considerations have their effect on the situation. The hastily-made MS staccato dot is easy to mistake for the $\mathbf{v}$ sign (accent +staccato); Berlioz's short *decrescendi* have been mistaken for accents, by both editors and players. As regards the use of the three accent marks, suspicion often arises that a symbol has vanished from a composer's scores because he has moved to a different publisher with a different house-style.

The line
Within a single work, this mark may be used in many senses:

Elgar: Enigma Variations

1. Held out + ritenuto? 2. Held out, no ritenuto? 3. Slight accent? 4. Slight separation? 5. Vibrato?

As Gardner Read suggests, the common factor in all uses is to give the effect of leaning on a note – to give it stress (generally) without accent.[39] No more precise definition is possible. It is the combination of sign *and context* that gives the clue for action. So, in word-language, we could say that a woman was like a cat, meaning that she was graceful, silent, spiteful to her friends, fond of milk, solitary, green-eyed. . . . . . .

Combined marks

All combinations may be used, as in

Vivacissimo $\downarrow$ = 176 - 168

Bartók: Mikrokosmos 146

Notice that the effect of these marks may be psychological as much as practical. The combined mark ♪̂ for piano can only mean *piu forte: sempre staccato*. The mark is used at a speed where no noticeable lengthening is possible. The combined 'accent; staccato; hold well out' (for which less than a fifth of a second is allowed) is impossible to interpret literally. It is a paradoxical notation, directing the performer simultaneously in opposite directions.

Slurs

The slur has an immediate practical use, and a less direct expressive use:

1) It may indicate bowing or breathing, or suggest a legato mode of performance.
2) It may divide up music to display the 'sense', affecting the mode of performance only indirectly.

84

Till about the middle of the eighteenth century, uses of the slur were restricted by the convention that slurring only rarely ran across the barline. Once it became acceptable practice to extend slurs freely, new uses developed. Phrasing may amplify or contradict symmetries or oppositions already suggested by phrase-lengths or harmonic structure, as follows (quoted by Keller[40]):

Freer uses introduce some ambiguities into the system. A slur over a string part may now *either* mean 'play in a single bow' or 'play without perceptible breaks as though in one bow':

Slurs in combination with staccato may be used to indicate a thematic cohesion – a paradoxical realization in which gaps are first created, then 'thought across' as the music is played:

'Expressive' uses can coexist with practical uses to suggest bowing, tonguing, note-fusion, or separation. Paired notes under a slur may carry the implication of a stress on the first note, a shortening of the second:

Refinements of nuance can be suggested by the use of slurs *under* slurs;

sometimes of slurs *under* slurs *under* slurs:

These markings are nothing if not subtle, and it is doubtful if any two players would exactly agree on their interpretation. The Berlioz marking might be taken to imply an expressive accent, a falling away on the second note, and a legato over the whole. How should we read the three slurs of the Mahler example? And why, at this same point, do the violins have the same passage with the uppermost slur omitted? The different phrasings Mahler gives to wind and strings in his scores are endlessly instructive, and only occasionally as puzzling as this.

Lastly, there is the slur which is also a tie – a marking originating with Beethoven, which seems to imply a felt division within a note, and perhaps a falling-away from first to second note:

Beams

The common, everyday use of beaming is to group notes according to metrical sense; the gain in clarity is obvious if we compare a vocal passage using un-beamed notes (the usual practice up to the 1940s was to follow the syllables of the text), with its modern equivalent:

86

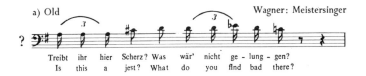

a) Old   Wagner: Meistersinger

Treibt ihr hier Scherz? Was wär' nicht ge - lung - gen?
Is this a jest? What do you find bad there?

Try to read this in correct rhythm; then reverse page for simplified modern equivalent.

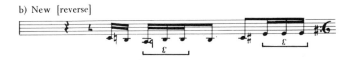

b) New [reverse]

Beams can also be extended, logically and helpfully, to include rests, assigning them to their proper beats:

Rudiments books were still making beat-by-beat beaming one of the absolute rules of good notational practice up to the last few years, but composers have for many years ignored the supposed rule with the greatest freedom. Beams, like slurs, have acquired a freedom that allows them to pass across the barline, or to establish independent patterns within the bar. In doing so, they have taken over some of the functions of the slur. Beamings may indicate phrasing, point up thematic relationships, create new metrical groupings. 'The deeply meaningful play of beams', as Schenker called it,[41] has become an important factor in the articulation of music. Because the beam has no first use as a directive to action, none of the doubts that arise in the case of the slur can exist; for with the slur, we can only judge from the context whether the mark is giving a specific instruction (play in one bow, or without tonguing), or informing us as to the sense in which we are to understand a phrase. There are, of course, other problems. It often happens that use of a beam to show phrasing or thematic relationships will make it harder to read the underlying beats. In regular situations, confusion need not arise; but where rhythms are irregular, great discretion must be observed:

a)

Copland: Statements

4 + 3 + 3

a) Beaming indicates an additive rhythm against a regular $\frac{3}{4}$.

Bartók: 3rd Quartet

b) ① Beaming warns against accenting intermediate beats.
   ② Beaming clarifies pattern of imitation.

c)   Tippett: Vision of St. Augustine

c) Beaming suggests irregular articulation pattern.

Bartók: Mikrokosmos 143

d)

d) Beaming clarifies the motivic construction; slur suppresses articulation.

88

Do any of the beamings in the previous examples clarify compositional processes at the price of making things harder for the player? The notator should at least be aware of the risk – that he may, in giving the directive, give elaborate demonstrations of compositional skills which have no relevance to the playing situation.

Beaming can also be used to reinforce the slur mark, separation being associated with un-beamed notes. This method is used, rather inconsistently, by Messiaen (who in most contexts beams conventionally by metric group):

Messiaen: Chronochromie

(Why are separate viola notes in lower line beamed in the fourth bar?)

Recent developments

New signs abound, some of them ambiguous. Stravinsky's use of $\bar{\rho}$ to stand for 'sharp attack without accent' (without staccato significance) is duly explained in some scores; in others, it appears without explanation, and doubts may arise as to its interpretation.

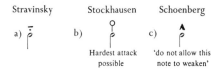

Donald Martino, perturbed by the vagueness of the line, has proposed a whole new set of 24 symbols to cover various types of attack, accent, and decay.[42]

PHONETIC REPRESENTATION	DESCRIPTION	SUGGESTED SYMBOLOGY	COMBINED SYMBOLS
1 ta, (ka/ga)	incisive, crisp attacks	•	ↄ) tap
1a pa, (ba/ma) 2 da, (na/la)	weak, delicate attacks	◡ —	•— tad
2a ha, (ja, wa) 3 (e/o), a	minimized, barely audible or non-existent attacks.	⊢ ⟍	◡—pad etc.)

If the aim is to tie down the performer to a precise interpretation, the 24 symbols are already both too many and still too few. Too many, because the increase in the number of signs to be recognized and responded to strains the already heavily-engaged attention of the performer; too few because such a range cannot begin to cover the countless subtle shades of inflection to be discovered in performance according to context and the particular circumstances prevailing. There is still room in music for an evocative, as well as a scientifically precise, notation. The ambiguity of (especially) the line ⌡ both involves the player in decision-taking and economically allows one sign to serve several purposes.

12 *Mood, Sense, and Silence*

Word directives

The symbols of notation are in the main concerned with the point-by-point conduct of the performer. If we want to speak generally of the understanding and articulation of phrases and sentences, we make use of slurring and beaming, finding secondary uses for symbols that had originally a limited and precise range of meaning. To speak more generally still of the over-all understanding of sense or structure, we must use words, accepting the dangers of imprecision, or lack of conciseness, arising from the use of non-specialist tools. The most useful mood-directives are those with a long history of past uses: dolce, espressivo, cantabile, have become, in effect, genuine musical terms. They carry with them rich background associations, and we can accordingly respond to them knowingly and predictably. Word-directives which have not been shaped and worn by long use need to be handled with great care. The single word at the head of a piece can encourage the performer to view the work through a single pair of spectacles. Vagueness as to what the composer understands by fantastico, serioso, daintily, jauntily . . . will often lead to the performer doing no more than play the notes and ignore the instruction. Instructions applied to the single phrase may be of detailed explicitness ('sharp, fast, clear, nervous' for trumpets in Copland's *Music for Theatre*), mock-humorous ('somewhat galumphing', Anthony Gilbert), or simply meaningless: in an orchestral tutti in Delius's *Eventyr*, where the whole orchestra is playing fortissimo, dotted semibreves in violins and violas – and these alone – are marked 'plaintively'. Often, instructions are clear but tautological. How *else* could the example below be played but scherzando; and how could many of Elgar's obviously noble tunes be played except nobilmente?

Stravinsky: Orpheus

Special signs

Traditionally, notation speaks authoritatively to the performer, telling him to 'do this' or 'do that', and shunning ambiguous meanings. If it were to distinguish between important and *un*-important, this would be as much as to say 'all instructions are to be obeyed, but some are to be obeyed more than others'. Yet, if we are to perform adequately, we must read through the notes to the sense behind; recognize leading themes; distinguish decorative from structural elements. There are various ways in which composer or editor may help the performer to find the sense of the music. Eighteenth-century ornament notation separated out structural from decorative elements; the elementary visual metaphor of LARGE and small can be used to suggest importance and unimportance, in the notation of appoggiaturas and graces. (It is interesting that Stockhausen respects tradition so far as to retain small noteheads for the many crushed-note figures of his keyboard music, while emphasizing, in a written instruction, that all notes are to be regarded as equally important.) Chopin's occasional practice of picking out the melody in big notes can be regarded as an extension of appoggiatura practice:

Etude no. 13, op. 25, no. 1

Markings that indicate leading parts suggest to the player that it is for him to find the right degree of emphasis to make the relative importance of parts clear to the listener:

Schoenberg: 3rd Quartet

H = Hauptstimme (principal part)
N = Nebenstimme (subsidiary part)

Several points can be made about this extract: that the special signs reinforce a meaning already implicit in dynamics; that such fine dynamic shadings can only suggest an interpretative attitude, that the 'poco scherzando', as in the earlier Stravinsky example, adds little of practical value. It is interesting to notice that Schoenberg very rarely felt a need for his *nebenstimme* marking; in this movement, *hauptstimme* is used 43 times, *nebenstimme* once only.

Of mood directions in general, it can be said that to use any marking that *could* be interpreted in action is almost to guarantee that it *will* be interpreted in action. Performers can only respond quickly and consistently if they establish regular reaction patterns. Where mood-words of broad connotation are used, the meaning generally gets narrowed down to imply a particular physical response. In this way, allegro long ago lost all implications of 'cheerfulness', and means simply 'fast'. Grandioso comes to mean louder, and probably slower; espressivo may be interpreted as con vibrato (and perhaps a little louder), and deciso, with more distinct attack.

Notation of silence

The idea of silence is as important to the musician as the idea of zero to the mathematician. Since the system of silence-notation exactly follows that of sound-notation, no serious problems exist that have not already been mentioned. Only the absence of beaming and grouping causes minor inconvenience (but see the example on p. 87 for a means of indicating the grouping of rests). In music, as in life, it often happens that instructions *not* to do are of the utmost importance. The orchestral player must *not* play in the silent bar; the traffic must *not* move when the traffic lights are at red. So we may find that instructions to inhibit action are heavily reinforced; the red traffic light by the superimposed *stop*, the duration of the rest by a double or triple notation:

a) The bar is empty; a rest is nevertheless added.
b) Graphical rest signs are reinforced by number.
c) Both rest sign and GP (general pause) confirm empty bar.

The instruction *not* to do, so vital to performers, is of no direct interest to conductors and score-readers. In recognition of this fact, the score has begun to rid itself of redundant rest symbols. Staves may share rests, and empty bars may be eliminated:

93

a) No staves where instruments are not playing.
b) No rest in empty bar.
c) Rests between staves.

Rests may have psychological rather than practical significance. The empty bar at the end of Beethoven's Piano Sonata, op. 31, No. 1, we may take to stand for the breathless hush with which Beethoven hopes the music will be received. The sophisticated modern equivalent of this marking can be found at the end of Messiaen's *Chronochromie*: two empty bars, of $\frac{3}{16}$ and $\frac{2}{16}$ respectively.

Warnings: What is not said
Negative instructions may be issued because it is easier to note exceptions to a general course of action ('Closed on Sundays' is more concise than 'Open on Mondays, Tuesdays, Wednesdays, etc.') So, when a generally expressive style of playing prevails, we need only notate the occasional senza espressione. With the change in playing habits that has brought vibrato into constant use, we need only notate non vibrato; in earlier ages, we would have notated the exceptional vibrato. The dance band orchestrator needs to notate both vibrato and arco for the double-bass player, whose everyday style is pizzicato e non vibrato. Many redundant markings – 'non cresc.', 'sempre piano', and Sibelius's $f\ldots\ldots f$, must be read as warnings. They indicate lack of confidence that the performer will carry out instructions already given, or implicit in previous markings. Excessive anxiety that the player shan't do the wrong thing leads to the situation found in Berg's *Lyric Suite*, where every note carries an accidental, regardless of what has gone before:

The *absence* of a directive, positive or negative, is not necessarily a sign that the player is free to do as he likes. We do not normally find in the streets notices telling us to drive on the appropriate side of the road, or not to commit murder. We do not find in music directives as to acceptable tone quality or the amount of latitude we are expected to take in inflecting time and pitch values. The absence of a directive may indicate that:

1) Everyone is presumed to be familiar with the appropriate convention.
2) It is a matter of indifference to the writer how that aspect of the music is represented.
3) An area of interpretation is regarded as the province of the performer.
4) Certain matters are left for viva voce instruction (when the writer is in charge of rehearsal).
5) The writer wishes to stimulate the performer by withholding information (see p. 75 for Cardew's explanation of unmarked dynamics).
6) The writer accepts the fact that the performer is not open to influence (no practical composer will notate a march for brass band as precisely as Mahler notated his symphonies).
7) Many aspects of sound cannot be exactly specified in any conventional written notation (see p. 78 on the notation of timbre).

13 *Auxiliary Notations*

Some of the instructions in a score may be concerned with the mechanics of performance rather than directly with the production of sound. Seating plans for the orchestra, or for the arrangement of a percussionist's instruments, may be found in many recent scores, including some by Stravinsky, Bartók, and Stockhausen. Wiring diagrams are given in electronic scores, detailed instruction for special preparation of instruments in some avant-garde scores (see Chapter 18). Conductors may be shown how to beat certain irregular rhythms (as in Stravinsky's *Dumbarton Oaks*); Boulez specifies details of conducting techniques, indicating left-hand signals to bring in groups of players independently, particular gestures to control crescendi and decrescendi. Special signs are used for divisions within irregular bars:

Cues and special markings may be included in individual parts to help players to coordinate. In the case of very complex music, these cues may take the form of a continuous cue-line part, above the player's own:

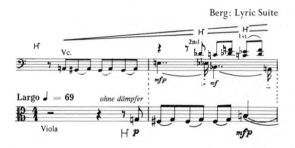

Berg: Lyric Suite

Difficult-to-read combinations in the score may be clarified, to help the conductor or score-reader to a better understanding. In the following, Elliot Carter gives the 'motive' of a passage under the full score:

Elliot Carter: 2nd Quartet

Various other auxiliary markings are ostensibly designed as aids to understanding, such as the arrows in some American study scores, which tell the reader to which line he should attend at any moment; the dotted lines connecting the notes of a tone-row dispersed among different parts; the harmonic 'directs' in Bruckner's scores, which forecast, at the bottom of each right-hand page, the immediate harmonic future course of the music. These concealed programme notes, love-calls to analysts and fellow-composers, have no practical value, though they may have autobiographical interest. Messiaen's naming of the birds in his birdsong-inspired works and his markings of the 'introversions', appeal in like manner over the heads of the performer to the score-reader. While it may possibly help the oboist in Beethoven's *Pastoral* Symphony to know that he is playing a quail, no xylophonist is likely to play better, or differently, when he knows that he is playing half of a Japanese Bird of Paradise.

Music can be 'explained', according to the views of the notator, in specially devised notations. These may take the form of vivid, graphical representations of the 'essential shapes' of music, as in Jeremy Johnson's notations for a BBC television series, produced by Nancy Thomas. The notation is specifically intended for a roller caption running horizontally past a cursor with the musicians in action superimposed:

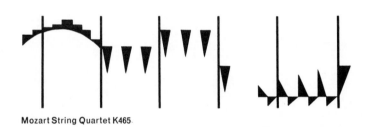

Mozart String Quartet K465.

97

Or they may concern themselves, more seriously, with deep structural and overall relationships:

a) Tracing a motive in Tchaikovsky's 6th Symphony according to Reti.[43] The 'theme' in the third extract is, of course, inaudible in performance:

b) Skeleton analysis of the opening of Schubert's B flat trio, D898 (Salzer[44]):

c) Analysis by Andrew Imbrie of Roger Sessions's Quintet (1958) (*P.N.M.* i, 1):

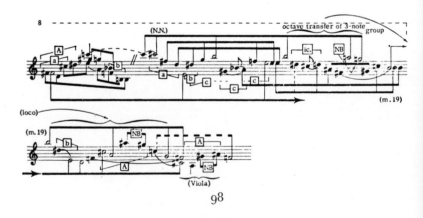

We need to remember that all analytical notations are necessarily selective, emphasizing or belittling this or that structural feature according to the viewpoint of the analyst. All such statements must be read as personal statements rather than objective simplifications of the notational equation. So Mainardi, in his edition of Bach's cello suites, gives two versions of the music – one for performance (A), the other giving his view of the music's underlying structure (B) (neither corresponds to the original text):

Bach: Suite II
(Allemande)

Teaching notations

Teaching notations are generally devised to solve the problems of special groups of learners, and are commonly thought of as stepping stones to the use of conventional systems. The action notations for recorders already described come into this category, as do the many 'singers' notations', mostly descended from the medieval *gamut*, designed to teach children the intervals of the scale and to help them pitch notes correctly. The gamut comprised a complicated arrangement of overlapping hexachords, used in conjunction with manual signs, the fingers and fingerjoints being used to stand for the hexachords, and individual notes that made up the complete gamut. A diagrammatic 'teaching hand' is shown on the next page:

99

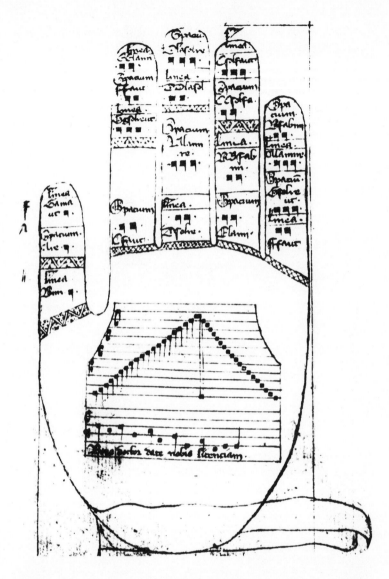

Of the many singers' notations derived from the gamut, and using alphabetic or numerical symbols to identify notes, tonic solfa has established itself firmly in use. Until lately, indeed, there were many amateur choirs who could read only from solfa notation. Its great advantage as a teaching method lies in its use of a 'movable *do*', the notes of the diatonic scale being always given the same names whatever the pitch. By this means, the different functions and characteristics of the notes of the scale are identified and labelled, rather than actual pitches – often far less significant to the singer. (The French system of fixed *do* solfeggio, by contrast, encouraged the development of pitch memory, since each sound is identified with the unvarying syllable to which it is sung.) The example (a) below summarizes the advantages of the system:

Advantages:

1) Notates identically in all keys (*).
2) Preserves identity of octave (†).
3) Observes different 'feel' of intervals in different parts of the scale (§).
4) Reminds user of different 'feel' of each note.
5) Can be written or sung, so that the need for a double system of symbols and call-words does not arise.

The main disadvantages are: the lack of graphical representation and the fact that Solfa is firmly tied to a diatonic system. It can indicate passing chromatics, but free modulation leads to constant and confusing shifting of ground, as the *do* moves from pitch to pitch:

The notation of minor keys is unsatisfactory (Schubertian major-minor fluctuations can only be shown to be a misleading shift of tonic). In atonal situations, the notation has no relevance.

By use of the 'modulator' – a chart (like an upright ruler) on which the symbols can be visually ordered – solfa teachers can supply the graphical representation missing in the notation. Its inventors tried also to establish the 'feel' of each note in the scale by naming and by use of associated hand signs (a traditional teaching method of long standing):

Do, Tonic, 'the STRONG or *firm* tone,' fist closed, horizontal, thumb down

Re, Second, 'the ROUSING or *hopeful* tone,' fingers extended, hand forming half a right-angle with ground, *back of hand* downwards

Mi, Major third, 'the STEADY or *calm* tone,' fingers extended, hand horizontal and back of hand undermost

Fa, Fourth, 'the DESOLATE or *awe-inspiring* tone' . . . . . .

Various attempts have been made to combine the graphical advantages of staff notation with the advantages of a notation that differentiates between the notes of the diatonic scale:

In today's context, the interest of such notations is only historical, for notations that are closely linked to the grammatical structure of music inevitably pay the price of specialization when the grammar undergoes radical alteration. It is *because* staff notation is reticent as to the syntax of music that we can still use it in situations where individual tones are put together on principles that were undreamt of fifty, or even twenty years ago.

A new approach to class teaching, pioneered in England by George Self and Brian Dennis, has led to the evolution of special systems which dispense with conventional stave and time notation. The main purposes of the new teaching methods are: to involve all children in musical activities rather than only the few who are laboriously acquiring conventional skills on conventional instruments; to delimit the field of *musical sounds* by suggesting free use of any available sound-sources; and to encourage experiment and controlled improvisation. Contemporary attitudes are reflected in the use made of pitched and unpitched percussion, and in notations which take over many of the methods and devices of notable avant-garde composers: proportionate time notation; grid notations; high, middle, and low specified rather than actual pitches; coordination by signal; 'free' signs to be subjectively interpreted by the performer (with or without reference to a time-pitch axis). Many of these features are shown below:

Brian Dennis: Experimental Music in Schools, Material no. 7

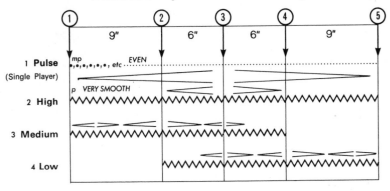

Because such notations illustrate the sounds simply and directly, children can learn to use them very quickly, moving on after only a few lessons to the performance of independent coordinated parts, and to the creation of their own music. Through these simplified performing techniques and notations, the way can be opened to new sorts of musical experience. Yet the problem (if it is a problem) remains – that these new activities, with their performing techniques and notations, remain apart from more conventional musical activities – not surprisingly when they imply a rejection of many of the attitudes and values of conventional educators. They offer, at present, an alternative or supplementary sort of musical education, unconnected with the normal 'musical activities' of schools and training colleges.

One last group of teaching notations should be mentioned: those designed as introductions to the understanding of conventional staff notations, being in fact notations of notations. The many musical games and fairy stories with which Victorian teachers used to sugar the pill of learning were often far-fetched and ingenious, and included what would not be called 'play-material'; such solid notational symbols as Dr. Rest's Musicland Bricks (see p. 104), sold at the Kindergarten warehouse, were worked into elaborate allegories covering every detail of the notational scheme from prolongation by dot to hemidemisemiquavers:

103

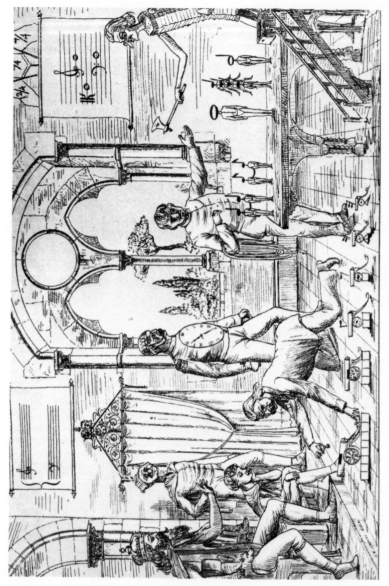

DR. REST EXHIBITING HIS CANNONS.

14 *Specialist Notations*

In two fields of activity, unrelated to the familiar areas of use, special notations have been evolved for special uses. Few readers are likely to be actively concerned in the notation of folkmusic of alien cultures or of electronic music; but the uses of notation in these fields raise some interesting questions, and force us to re-think basic problems. In either case, we start with a clean slate. There are no traditions of interpretation to be respected, no established systems. In notating descriptive scores of folk-music, the notator has to discover not simply how far he can go in showing detail, but how far he wants to go. In notating electronic music, he is also faced, in issuing the directive, with the problem of total determinacy. Where interpretation is, literally, mechanical, all must be specified. When we move into either of these fields, we have to revise our ideas on the definition of notes, intervals, and significant dimensions of sound. It becomes clear that the divisions of conventional systems are arbitrary, made for our own convenience, and conforming to no grand universal system. Words, it has been said, are what are listed in dictionaries; and *notes*, whether sounding or written, are what we have decided to perceive or write as notes. 'The categories and types that we isolate from the world of phenomena we do not find there because they stare every observer in the face ... we cut nature up, organize it into concepts, and ascribe significances largely because we are parties to an agreement to organize it that way.'[46]

a) ETHNOMUSICOLOGISTS' NOTATIONS

In one field, the descriptive score is of great importance. The ethnomusicologist, collecting music performed by non-literate musicians, works back from the sounding music to a notated version that aptly describes the sounds heard or recorded. His description, while it can never be complete, aims to give a faithful account of a particular performance. 'All we can say is that then and there, at the time of that performance, it proved to be such' Bartók writes of his Serbo-Hungarian folk-song transcriptions.[47] A good ethnomusicologist, in fact, does much more than provide a faithful description – he uses notation to select, to differentiate, to reach an understanding of the principles of organization, establishing the difference between significant and insignificant. He aims, in his notation, to follow the structure of the language of the music he is transcribing.

Before recording devices came into use, traditional music was of necessity written down on the spot – a method still used by some collectors, who value the prolonged and intimate contact established in the process between performer and collector. Early collectors almost invariably used conventional notation, often leading to grotesque results where exotic musics were forced into a Western mould. As comparative musicology developed into a serious study, a strong reaction took place. The experts, instead of looking for similarities, denied any connection between Western and non-Western musics.* These extreme views are no longer tenable. Similar patterns of tonal construction *are* shared; the pentatonic scale, for instance, is found in N. Asia, Negro Africa, and among the American Indians, as well as in all parts of Europe. There are, then, many situations in which conventional notation can be used to show without distortion certain aspects of the music described. With a few modifications and additions, we can show in some detail inflection, mode of passing from note to note, and suggest distinctions between structural and decorative elements:

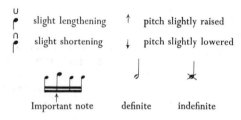

⌣♪	slight lengthening	↑	pitch slightly raised
⌢♪	slight shortening	↓	pitch slightly lowered

Important note   definite   indefinite

Bartók & Lord: Serbo-Croatian Folk-Songs

* Hornbostel's basic premise was that tribal music discloses structural principles entirely opposed to those governing Western music, and that in the vocal music of African tribes 'typically, melodic steps are very small, amount-

This extract from the Bartók-Lord transcription shows the method at its most conscientious and detailed. Such a thorough transcription is only possible when transcribers work from recordings – often from slowed-down playbacks. The limitation of the method lies in its analytical bias. A western 'one pitch-one symbol' notation can only represent music as a series of separate sound events, with the fixed-pitch tone as the significant unit. Bartók's detailed notation makes no distinction, for instance, between a narrow trill (alternation of two tones) and a wide vibrato (a single fluctuating tone). Yet there is a wide conceptual difference between the two, and a notation that renders both impartially is linguistically unhelpful. A more extreme example would be the notation of the wavering plucked notes of the Indian sitar player. The transcriber into conventional notation would have no choice but to represent the sound as a series of distinct sound-events, whereas a truer notation would record a single sound-event.

The alternative is to make a fresh start, representing melody as a contour on a time-pitch graph. The method has certain advantages. Melody can be represented as a continuum of sound; a stream rather than a series of isolated events. We are no longer directed by the notation to perceive the music in a certain way, by imposing on the music a fixed-step structure or an implication of divisive rhythm. Two objections can be raised: that a graphical notation is too impartial, and sidesteps the real issue – on what principles is the music organized? – and that we have to find a compromise between notations suitable to the music, and notations that are accessible to readers.

Uses of conventional and graphical notation are not, fortunately, mutually exclusive. They may be used to give different types of information, or the notator could, conceivably, switch from one to the other after the manner of Berio. The example on p. 108 shows three transcriptions, made from a recording, of a single extract from a Hukwe song with drum accompaniment, version 1 using a form of graphical notation for the voice part. Notice the variants that appear; they do not indicate a 'correct' or 'incorrect' version so much as a difference of opinion as to how detailed the notation can usefully be. Are the upper drum tones shown in versions 2 and 3 a significant feature or not? The aim of the transcriber is not simply to provide a faithful record, but

ing, at most, to a major third or so. But within this small group, no distinctions are made: a 'third' is not different in function from a second, and the width of an interval can vary time after time within wide margins'.[48]

to separate essential from inessential; to show an appropriate amount of detail while avoiding meaningless precision and to reflect in the structure of the notation the way in which the performers 'think' the music.

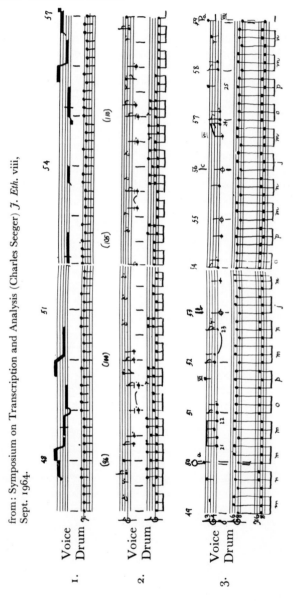

from: Symposium on Transcription and Analysis (Charles Seeger) *J. Eth.* viii, Sept. 1964.

Two devices, one theoretical and one practical, for the objective description of performed music are of some importance to the comparative musicologist. The first is the logarithmic scale for interval measurement. In the familiar Western context, we can refer to thirds, fourths, or fifths, the terms standing for 'the intervals that we all recognise as thirds, fourths, or fifths'. In describing alien musics, we often need to specify intervals in the scale exactly. For this purpose, the system of Cents evolved by A. J. Ellis is generally used. All intervals within the octave are represented on a logarithmic scale from 0 to 1,200 (giving a value of 100 cents for the equal temperament semitone). Interval numbers in cents can be added or subtracted (whereas frequency ratios have to be multiplied or divided). A linear relationship is established between the sizes of different intervals, so that a direct comparison can be made between intervals within the scale or between different scales. Using a logarithmic scale, intervals may be represented graphically, an interval being represented by the same length whatever its position in terms of pitch level:

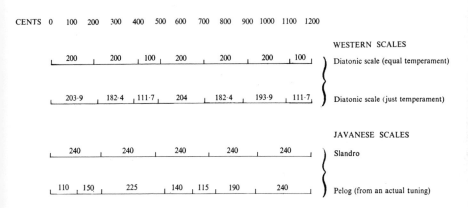

The second, recent innovation has been the development of automatic melody writers used by Seeger in America, and by Dahlback and Bengtsson at Oslo and Uppsala. These electronic devices can produce a time-pitch graphical record of monophonic music, on any desired scale. The following example shows the opening of 'La Marseillaise'.

Melody Registration. First line of 'La Marseillaise', played on a flute; from Bengtsson[49].

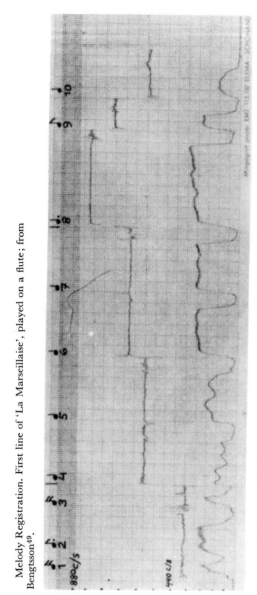

lower graph shows amplitude

The attraction of automatic transcription lies in the elimination of the human, subjective element since any transcriber's perception habits are likely to influence the way in which he hears, and so notates, unfamiliar music. To describe the melograph as an 'automatic music notator', as Seeger does, is nevertheless going rather far: a meaningful notation must concern itself not only with the physical sound-events, but with the way in which they are conceived and organised. The melograph may suggest 'what happens between the notes', but, since it operates by suppressing all partials above the fundamental, naturally gives no information on timbre or many other potentially interesting aspects of a performance. It has, even so, been objected that these wave traces provided too much information. It would be truer to say that the information is not yet in meaningful form; but as Bengtsson points out,[49] use of the melograph does not deprive us of existing methods of selection. What it can provide, and most usefully, is unweighted evidence, on the basis of which we can read, measure, and interpret.

We can now (following Bengtsson) list some of the questions that the ethnomusicologist needs to answer in arriving at an appropriate notation:

1) What are the 'essential' qualities of the material? (Do they involve pitch, rhythm, timbre, manner of attack, or movement between tones?)
2) What scale of calibration is appropriate
   a) to the purposes of the notator (to show overall structure or detail)?
   b) to the nature of the music (meaningless overprecision must be avoided)?
3) How far is the notation to be generalized to represent an average, or ideal, performance?*
4) What is the nature of the unit to be separated for study? (Can any unit be separated for study?)
5) Who is to read the notation?†

* 'Unless we are specifically studying interpretations, we want to know what a musician sets out to do each time he plays a piece of music, not *exactly* what he did on one particular occasion.' J. Blacking[50]
† 'Description . . . must above all be communicative and make some concessions to the reader's frame of reference.' C. Seeger[51]

b) NOTATION OF ELECTRONIC MUSIC

Many patterns of communication and cooperation may be involved in the production of electronic music. At the lowest level, the composer may approach the technician without specialist knowledge of the medium; Stravinsky envisages the type of direction given: 'something electronic, kind of middle range, bassoon-trombone like'.[52] At higher levels, collaboration between composer and technician will be close, with back-and-forth exchange of ideas and influence. The line of demarcation between the two will rarely be clearly observed, for the composer must be himself something of a technician if he is to grasp the possibilities of the medium, and will often act as his own technician. In the so-called 'classical' studio, control over all operations of sound generation, modification, recording, and editing remains in the hands of human operators. In computerized studios, the computers take over many of the more laborious tasks. They can combine processes previously carried out separately and at great expense of time into a single operation. They can accept and store information and instructions as to procedures in many different forms; can themselves generate sounds, and take decisions, according to present conditions, to produce further data or a final realization in sound. A further possibility exists: the composer may draw a picture of the sound wave, which can be transferred to tape and played direct.

In all cases, the situation is an experimental one, involving new sounds, new relationships between participants, and new notational needs and problems. Old ideas as to what constitutes a note vanish, together with the limited vocabulary of known referents (the pitches, durations, and graded dynamic values of traditional music). Gone too is the need for a formal directive, addressed at large to the hypothetical performer. In the field of mechanically produced music, the need for repeated performances and the specification to produce them no longer exists: the tape of the work is the permanent performance, repeatable ad infinitum. (The special case of computer-composed works will be considered later.)

The composer, then, is in the position of the scientific experimenter. He is likely to work to a definite plan of action. He may well produce copious informal work notes as he proceeds, but these are intended for immediate use, not for publication. Only when the experiment is successfully completed will he produce the final writing up. Theoretically, it is possible for the exact specification to be drawn up before realization begins; in practice, revisions and modifications will be called for while work is in progress, for in our present state of knowledge results cannot be exactly predicted.

The scores of early electronic music generally had the appearance of conventional double-purpose scores, combining a detailed description of the way in which the sounds were (or could again be) produced, with some kind of graphical representation of the way in which they might be expected to sound. They generally combine a frequency chart with a chart for dynamics, and are accompanied by notes on methods of sound generation, notes on tape-manipulating processes, wiring diagrams, and pages of frequency tables. Where the composer deliberately limits himself to simple methods of sound generation and a few basic elements, specification can be complete, and the graphical score can provide a meaningful map or model of the sounds to be heard. Stockhausen's *Elektronische Studien II* provides an example (see overleaf). Where more complex processes are involved, the business of defining fully either the sounds or the means by which they are to be produced becomes very difficult and very laborious. The score of Dobrowolski's *Music for Magnetic Tape no. 1* carries with it a glossary to explain the different sources of sounds used, supplementary graphs to define the ways in which tone complexes are built up, frequency tables, and diagrams to illustrate the modifications brought about in natural patterns of attack and decay for sounds generated from natural sources. No lay listener is likely to be able to reconstruct the sounds in his imagination with any confidence from such a score; while the potential performer can turn to the recording conveniently included in a back pocket. It is difficult to see what purpose such a score serves, or what incentive exists for the re-realization of a score which has already been realized. Two other difficulties diminish any usefulness these scores have as directives. The first, that even in this field of absolute control, exactitude escapes the realizer. Peter Zinovieff points out that 'no two studios have the same precise calibration of their devices. One cannot obtain a signal of frequency absolutely 10,000.00 Hz, it must be give or take something.'[53] Next, that equipment and methods of work vary so much from studio to studio as to make it unlikely that a step-by-step instruction book will ever be of use to later musicians. The interest of such scores is historical – they provide documentation for what was done at a certain time and place.

Stockhausen: Elektronische Studien II

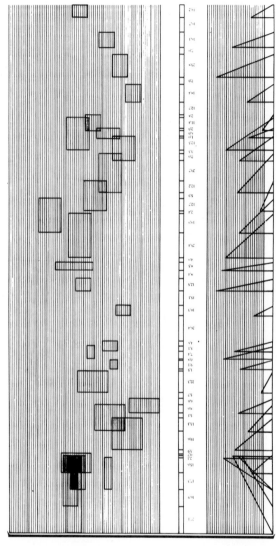

The upper half shows frequencies. Each block corresponds to one note, made up of five frequencies at constant intervals, of which the highest and lowest are shown. Overlapping mixtures are shown by heavier shading. On the intensity graph below, each note-mixture has a corresponding envelope of equal length. Durations are calibrated on the central line.

Descriptive scores

The need for descriptive scores in electronic music remains. Where there are no established conventions of organization and no familiar sounds with their attached associations, some handle to understanding is needed all the more urgently. Scores need to be produced in the form of sketch-maps: graphical programme notes, providing some sort of analogue for the sounds to be heard, and a lifeline for the listener, afloat in a strange sea. With increasingly sophisticated techniques of sound manipulation, the difficulty of finding any points of reference becomes continually greater. There are, all the same, certain basic elements and processes in common use, and these can be meaningfully symbolized. We are growing used to the names, and even to the characteristics in sound, of sine waves, saw-tooth, and square waves, at least in their simpler forms. Repetitions and symmetries can be pointed out in the notation; dense and spare textures, high and low, symbolized graphically. The score of Tristram Cary's *345 A Study in Limited Resources* (see overleaf) shows a combination of special symbols with conventional dynamic signs, a good deal of verbal explanation, and a glossary for the use of the uninformed. The concept of movement in space, here as so often an important structural element, is also shown. With the help of this score, fellow composers could deduce the type of music represented, and the listener might be able to keep his bearings during performance. It is still only a sketch map; only in cases where the composer has drastically limited his vocabulary and kept to simple methods of sound-processing can the score reflect more than a fraction of the content of the work.

The limited range of frequencies used, and the distribution in space, is indicated on the left of the score. The main symbols used to indicate the type of sound in use are:

◯	sine wave
△	saw-tooth wave
▢	square wave
▢ ┆ ◯	modulation of two sounds

Tristram Cary: 345

116

In works for live instruments with tape, a descriptive cue-line often needs to be given. In Stockhausen's *Kontakte* the cue can do little more than enable the reader to keep his bearings as the tape plays:

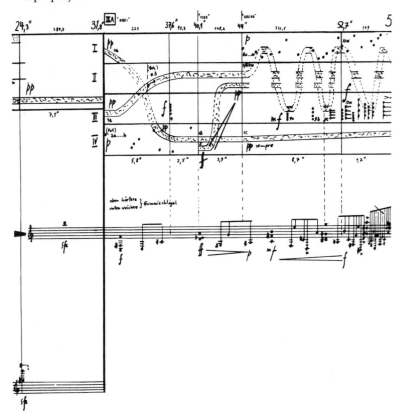

Computer notations

We must speak to each machine in the language it can understand. We instruct the musical box by pinned drum, the record player by grooved disc. The digital computer, essentially a sophisticated calculating machine with a memory, must be instructed in numbers. In the case of the electronic analog computer, which is used to solve problems involving variables, input is in the form of a continuously variable voltage.

The computer, unlike the musical box and the record player,

is a general purpose tool, for which many applications have been found. To increase its availability to non-specialists (that is, those who know more about the job in hand than the inner workings of the computer), many methods of input have been developed to supply a link between information the user can understand and information that can be understood by the computer's central processor. Optical recognition devices (such as the familar magnetic ink cheque-numbers readable by man or machine); graphs drawn with 'light pen' on fluorescent screen; instructions written in ordinary characters on paper, or printed in a type face the computer has been educated to read – all can be used as input; it is even possible for a computer to accept instruction from the human voice. For most every-day applications, input is by typewriter keyboard, the alphanumerical instruction in letters and numbers being translated into numerical machine code by assembler program. In this symbolic language, each instruction can be represented in a convenient mnemonic form, and the addresses or memory locations at which information is to be stored can also be given letter names. If a standard operation is to be used which involves the giving of several machine code instructions, these can be packaged together and a single instruction in the symbolic language can be used for the packaged operation (sub-routine). (If a mathematician wants to find a square root, he may need only to type TYPE SQRT (3), for the computer to translate into the number of machine code instructions necessary to produce the answer, which is typed out as the final output.)

Uses of the computer in music fall, at the moment of writing, into three categories: bibliographical, compositional (carrying out any instruction program that involves computation with notational symbols), and sound-generation (either by control of electronic equipment or by direct synthesis). In any of these applications, musical information in the form of conventional symbols may need to be fed into the computer. Where typewriter input is used, this involves a secondary coding operation so that symbols and positions can be represented alphanumerically. The following example[54] shows the type of substitution employed.

Allegro   Mozart: Piano Sonata no. 3, K 281

(All ♭BE24)y8. tB   3C D (6B A C)(B A E)   /(C B D)(C B 'F) 8Dz - /

Any conventionally notated music can be thus represented as a single series of letters and numbers, which the computer can translate into machine code. Thereafter, the computer can be programmed to operate on the number-sequence in any way that is desired. Subroutines may be written by which numbers of machine instructions are packaged together, as described above, so that a complex operation can be set off by a single instruction in the symbolic language.

All musical computer languages reflect the particular purposes for which they are developed. IML (intermediate music language) is a programming language for the storing of musical information. MIR (music information retrieval) is a language for programming and computing, designed 'to carry out any effectively music-theoretical propositional functions – i.e., any predicate whose truth value is computable from the notes', and has been used for various types of music-analysis. Both of these are assembly languages – that is, only available for the machines for which they were written (the IBM 7094). MUSIC IV, a program for generating electronic music developed at the Bell Laboratories, has been rewritten in Fortran, a programming language that contains no reference to any specific computer. (The high level languages are adapted to special needs rather than to special machines: COBOL for business uses, ALGOL and FORTRAN for scientific and technological uses, are among the most used. Each computer manufacturer translates the statements of the language into machine-code equivalent for his own computers.) MUSICOMP (written in SCAT, a standard machine language for the IBM 7090), is a compositional and sound-synthesizing language developed at the University of Illinois, and is conceived 'not as a fixed entity, but as an adaptable language that we expect to change and to expand as our programming experience mounts' (Lejaren Hiller). In MUSYS, the system developed at the Electronic Music Studio at Putney (London) by Peter Zinovieff, Peter Grogono, and David Cockerell, PDP8/L and PDP8/S computers are used to control special-purpose electronic music equipment (though the system includes facilities for waveform synthesis). The system as a whole is designed 'not to let computers compose, but to enable composers to use computers to minimize the chores of electronic composition' and the current language, MUSYS III, provides a means both to solve 'most of the structural, mathematical, and logical problems that may be encountered by musicians' and to control sound-production.

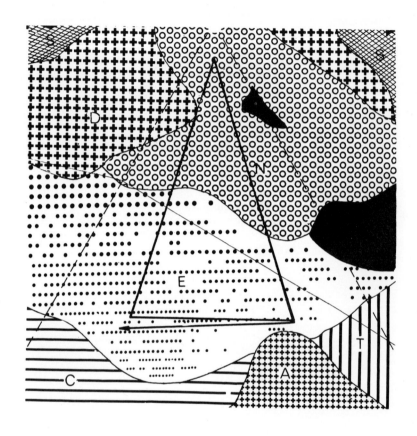

Part of the score of December Hollow by Peter Zinovieff

Shading
S- Surprise; T- Tension; E- Expectation; C- Catharsis;
N- Neutrality; A- Anxiety; D- Dependance; Solid Black- Boredom

Central Triangle - possible starting area
Thin Line - one integration

Reverse Side
A- a; B- Beautiful; C- Composition; D- Do; I- Is; M- Make or Me
P- Please; S- Suppose or So; T- Think or this

New methods of input may soon make it easier for non-specialists to program computers. An adaptation of the Graphos I, an engineering graphical input device, makes it possible to draw scores as graphical functions of time, and to hear the result played back at once: dynamics can be indicated on a secondary graph. 'The programs provide great flexibility for drawing, copying, erasing, and altering functions. Thus it is easy to develop a sound sequence by a series of trials.'[55] In theory, there is no reason why optical recognition devices should not be developed to accept printed or handwritten material in conventional or unconventional notation on paper. It should, all the same, be emphasized that sophisticated equipment and ease of handling does not inevitably lead to better musical results – over the whole field of electronic music, it is the quality of the operators, rather than the quality of machines, that counts for most.

What of the future of computer notations? It is likely that they will become less formal, more conversational. The computer will be able to question obscure directives, and itself to solve some of the problems of how problems should be attacked, so that the exact logical form of instruction will be relaxed. The connection with conventional notations will become less apparent, as it becomes clear to all that where any sound can be called for, in any terms, the old categorizations and restrictions no longer exist. 'In the end,' Peter Zinovieff suggests, 'we can each have our own private languages specially tailored for our own machines and individual needs or frustrations.'[53]

The example on p. 120 shows part of the score, or pre-compositional analysis, of Zinovieff's *December Hollow*. The names or areas (Boredom, Surprise, etc.) are convenient labels for types of activity worked out by the composer and computer in collaboration. The course of a possible performance could be charted as a single line passing across the map (which is in this case to be folded to form an open three-dimensional tetrahedron). The situation is parallel to that found in the game-compositions of avant-garde composers. Any number of realizations is possible, and each will conform to the overall system of control. The implication is that it is processes behind the sounds as much as the sounds themselves that constitute the music; a position that the computer-composer is prepared to uphold by notating the processes and leaving the sounds to look after themselves.

PART THREE Today and Tomorrow

In these final chapters, we deal with recent major developments in the notational situation, and suggest some connections between the line of evolution and the preoccupations and activities of our age. These are the four main points to be discussed:

1) The emergence, in a literate age, of intellectual and visual 'musics' derived from the written rather than the sounding music.
2) The increasing rigour of determinate notations, and consequent reduced status of the performer; leading to
3) Indeterminate music and the reinstatement of the performer.
4) Electronic music and the elimination of the performer.

15 *Literary Attitudes*

We can hear a given piece of music a hundred times and yet, if we do not know it also from the sight of the notes the composer has put on paper, get no further than the outer rim of his thought.

(Ernest Newman)[56]

You must distinguish from music the effects of rhythm, like e.g. a drum, and timbre of instruments . . . but that is not music . . . MUSIC is written on paper . . . it's the intervals etc. And these are intellectual not sensorial things.

(Barbara, ' a very musical amateur', quoted by Vernon Lee)[57]

The supreme joy of the musician is to take a score as the average man reads a book and to be able to hear the music as vividly and convincingly as the other follows the words of language.

(Ernest Fowles)[58]

One seeing is worth a hundred listenings.

(Chinese proverb)

In a literate age, respect for the written word or note stands high. Many come to think that the authentic message is somehow *in* the book or score, and that later realizations are only imperfect versions of ideal truth. Scholars may prefer to stay at home with the texts of Shakespeare's plays rather than risk the misinterpretations of the live theatre, and learned musicians may claim that the purest enjoyment and understanding comes from silent reading. From this point of view, the blurring resonances, the imperfections and approximations of live performance, confuse the issue; it is the ideal, abstract relationships, so clearly expressed on paper, that such listeners value.

In an age when the live sounds of music are continually brought home to us by radio and recording, we hear less of those ivory-tower musicians who love to sit quietly at home, listening to silent music. Yet it remains true that, in a literate age, music has a double character. Generalizing, we can say that we often find it easier to appreciate structural and intellectual qualities of a piece from a reading of the score, while the emotional impact is only made apparent in live performance. On the printed page, the processes of composition can be easily followed. We can refer backward and forward; parts can be simultaneously viewed, and where every detail is fixed, we can come to terms with music at our leisure. Often, the processes of composition may be appreciated as elegant or clumsy, have aesthetic or intellectual value, almost without reference to the resulting sounds, and we can appreciate the excellence and originality of the organization while remaining uninterested in the end-result. While practical musicians insist, with Schoenberg, that 'the ear is the musician's sole brain', we are often aware of this cleavage between music on paper, and music as sound. Copland has commented on the division in Schoenberg's own music: 'We are faced, then, with two seemingly opposite facts; on the one hand the music is carefully plotted in every detail; and on the other it undeniably creates an anarchic impression. On the one hand the musical journals of every country are filled with articles explaining the note-for-note logic of Schoenbergian music, accompanied by appropriate graphs, abstracts, and schematized reductions, enormous energy being expended on the tracking down of every last refinement in an unbelievably complex texture. (One gains the impression that it is not the music before which the commentators are lost in admiration so much as the way in which it leads itself to detailed analysis.) But, on the other hand, when we return to the concert hall and listen once again to these same compositions we leave with the disturbing memory of a music that borders on chaos.'[59] 'Chaos' is a strong word. But Copland wrote in 1951, at a time when performances were rarer, and under-rehearsal of the very difficult music heightened the impression of chaos.

In music based on more complex computational techniques –

serial music in which rows are split, dispersed, rotated, or combined; or in which all parameters are serialized; or in which results are reached by stochastic processes, the cleavage becomes greater still, and the listener can pick up no clues from the sounding music as to the organizing principles of composition. You may argue, with Cage, that 'composing's one thing, performing's another, and listening's a third. What can they have to do with one another?' In that case, the position has certainly changed. In previous ages, it was normally possible to trace composition processes by listening. Today, composers will warn listeners that the composition processes have nothing to do with them – so we apparently arrive at a position where two currents of interest, one intellectual and one sounding, flow independently to readers and listeners.

Eye music

'A musical notation that looks beautiful' Cardew has said, 'is not a beautiful notation, because it is not the function of a notation to look beautiful.'[35] Yet we do recognize a connection between the look and the sound of music, and it has often pleased composers to create musical puns, so arranging things that the look of the music reflects or foreshadows its sound, shape, or character. Medieval composers used red ink to set the word *blood*, green for *grass*; used black and white notes for *grief* and *joy*, *darkness* and *light*. Love-songs from the court of Avignon were written in the form of hearts or circles (see p. 125); there is a Byrd madrigal in which the words 'sourest sharps and uncouth flats' are set on a page bristling with the appropriate accidentals:

William Byrd: Come, woeful Orpheus

In much the same way, some of today's avant-garde composers search for a close equivalence between the look and the sound of music. For every literate musician, there is a strong tendency for every impression to translate itself into musical terms. In some cases, the translation is literal. Weber is supposed to have written the march in his *Turandot* after a late-night view of upturned chairs on cafe tables, which suggested the crotchets and quavers of the music. Schumann's letter cyphers (themes that spell out the names of friends in the letter-names of notes) are

124

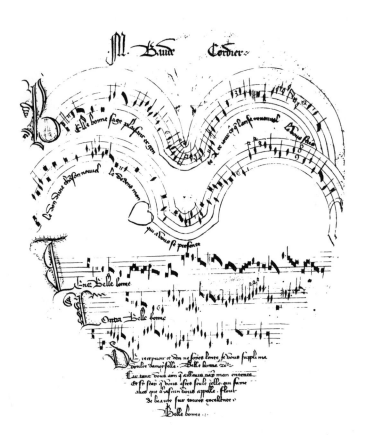

well known. An odder example is Charles Ives's sound-realization of a football game: 'Yale-Princeton Game, (August 1907). The wedge formation piece; notes set on paper like men on the football field – one note runs round left for a loss, etc. . . .'[60]

Kagel has used notation-manipulation to vary themes in different ways. In the examples given (from *Die Reihe*, no. 7), the final form of the music grows out of the form of the notation. Use of any other medium than the five-line stave would clearly give different results:

We list the following *coupled categories:*
Screwing, as a coupling of straight line and circular shifts around a screwing point and a constant axis of translation.

Rotation develops really as a changed principle of screwing—when one represents time as a (straight-line) sliding axis. If one hears successively the basic shape and a shape derived from it, this has the effect, temporally, of a turning in a certain direction.

Rotation and mirroring as a turning of the basic shape around one turning point and one mirror-axis.

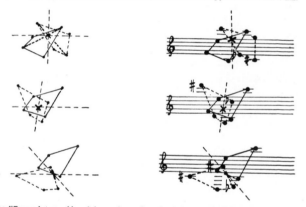

The difference between this and the usual sort of rotation is that here the derived shape turns on top of the basic shape.

Rotation and spreading as a circular and centripetal shift (with regular or irregular growth of the basic shape) around a *spiral axis*.

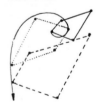

16 *Towards a Determinate Notation*

I have often said my music is to be 'read', to be 'executed', but not to be 'interpreted'.   (Stravinsky)[52]

The piece is so orchestrated (at least that was my intention) that the sound depends on the players playing exactly what I have written.
                                                            (Schoenberg)[61]

It gratifies me . . . how distinctly my music can speak to a true musician, he can know and understand me without explanations, simply through the medium of the written notes.   (Schoenberg)[61]

Composers like Stravinsky and Schoenberg leave the interpreter no freedom whatever; every nuance of dynamic, tempo, phrasing, rhythm and expression is rigidly prescribed, and the performer is reduced to the status of a gramophone record.   (Thurston Dart)[6]

Through the first half of the present century, the tendency has been for the composer to encroach on the freedom of the performer, extending control into areas where the performer had previously been free to take decisions, and specifying ever more exactly what is required. Many examples in the first half of this book have illustrated the move towards a high-definition notation, embodying the idea that if we could only get the right notation and the right players, the desired performance would automatically follow.

The composer's desire to take over responsibility for all aspects of performance can be accounted for in various ways. First of all, his own status has never stood so high. We live in an age of 'work-fidelity' (Krenek's phrase); of reverence for the urtext, and the principle that the composer has the moral right to be master in his own house. Many other causes contribute: the lack of a universal grammar of music, resulting in a situation where performers cannot necessarily understand what they are asked to do, and so must be shown step by step; the lack of personal contact, in an age of specialist composers often far from the scene of the performance, which necessitates a fuller written directive; reaction against nineteenth-century traditions of elastic interpretation. There are also two technical reasons why a highly determinate notation is appropriate to our age: the extreme concentration of much contemporary music demands an equally detailed notation, which will account for the music's microstructure with a painstaking thoroughness; and secondly, there is the question of the intelligence, skill, and availability of the new generation of contemporary performers, which open up new possibilities of getting ever more exacting instructions carried out. More generally, we should allow for the mechanistic, deterministic spirit of the age, which tends towards objectivity and clarity, putting no trust in that which cannot be measured.

Since the 1950s, the ideal of a totally determinate notation has become somewhat tarnished. It has grown increasingly clear that absolute control, mechanistic response, can never be attained while the human relationship is involved. Advocates of total determinacy failed to take account of four main factors:

1) The limits of the human performer.
2) The incompleteness of the notational specification.
3) The extent to which unconscious deviation from the directive contributes to satisfactory realization.
4) The inappropriateness of an authoritarian directive in contexts where creative collaboration is called for.

1) The limits of human perception and execution must not be overpassed. Failure to observe them led to the impossibly exacting notations of the earlier pointillist scores of Boulez and Stockhausen and involved us in the dilemma described by Lukas Foss: 'the precise notation which results in imprecise performance . . . to learn to play the disorderly in orderly fashion is to multiply rehearsal time by a hundred'[62].

2) Only since the development of electronic music, which compels the composer to define all aspects of sound, have we become aware of the incompleteness of conventional notation. Timbre, attack and decay, dynamic and tempo changes, are all vaguely specified. To do more is to put an impossible load on the composer as well as on the performer. Where, for instance, the timbre of a single oboe note may be varied in 98 ways by the use of different fingerings and methods of blowing, the composer may well decide that the time has come to restore some of the decision-making to the performer, in view of the huge extra load of specialist knowledge needed for full notation.

128

3) The descriptive registrations first used by Seashore in his researches on interpretative practices, and later developed by the ethnomusicologists, have made it easier for us to accept the extent of deviation in what we regard as normal, accurate, performance. Notation seems to tell us to perceive music in a certain way, so that we may think we are hearing exactly what we see, without realizing how much latitude is taken and allowed. What we recognize as a faithful performance is never a literal performance; and when we get a literal performance, we don't find it acceptable. Krenek can now write: 'I have repeatedly heard honest and talented musicians make a sorry caricature of a work in the modern idiom, despite the fact that they reproduced it literally and, from a technical viewpoint, unobjectionably.'[63]

4) The inappropriateness of the authoritarian directive, with its implication of a separation of functions between composer and performer, duly follows. 'The methodical division of labor (I write it, you play it) served us well until composer and performer became like the two halves of a worm, each proceeding obliviously on its way'.[62] In other words, literal, deadpan obedience is not enough. The performer's creative collaboration is essential. With understanding, he must read between the notes; establish the context in which signs are to be interpreted; and regulate all the minute variations of tone colour, articulation, and attack which can never be fully notated, and which are in many cases made intuitively rather than consciously.

The reaction against the more extreme forms of determinist notation has now spread even to the most convinced determinists of earlier times. Stockhausen and Boulez have become noticeably more permissive, and even Stravinsky relented: 'Some elements must always be transmitted by the performer, bless him.' Those who still demand an exact realization of their directives are now able to find an outlet in electronic music; a possibility already foreseen by Honegger* and Varèse in the 1920s. Together with disillusionment has come a greater understanding of the nature of the notational link. The old idea that notation was a straightforward, self-contained set of instructions, like the instructions for putting together a garden hut or operating an electric mixer, held

---

* 'The future is with the completely mechanical orchestra . . . by the development of machine made music . . . alone capable of solving the problems created by the growing demands of human interpreters.'
    'By suppressing them?'
    'Yes.'[10]

that all that was needed was to be clear, explicit, unambiguous – a view that leads to the oversimplifications of the notation experts:

'Why composers should not write out in full what they intended must remain a mystery. It would have saved a great deal of unnecessary trouble'

(Kitson)[64]

'The absolutely infallible principle of notation: be explicit' (Gardner Read)[39]

Today, we accept the fact that notation operates in the whole context of human behaviour, and that the subtlest psychological or aesthetic appeals and suggestions have their place in the system. The idea of notation as itself a creative activity underlies the often fanciful notations of today's avant-garde, and is itself a reaction against the stern objectivity of the preceding age. Contrast with the quotations at the beginning of this chapter Roberto Gerhard's view of the role of notation: 'Notation's ambiguities are its saving grace. Fundamentally, notation is a serviceable device for coping with imponderables. Precision is never of the essence in creative work. Subliminal man (the real creative boss) gets along famously with material of such low definition that any self-respecting computer would have to reject it as unprogrammable.'[65]

17 *Experiment and Reform*

Mensural notation of the sixteenth century.

Hindemith autograph (20th century)

During four hundred years of notational stability the main features of the notation map remained almost unchanged. The advantages of universal comprehension (extending back to the music of the past), of ease in writing and reading derived from constant use, to say nothing of the capital invested in printing and engraving equipment and unsold stock, decisively outweighed the remote gains offered by plans for reform. The very familiarity of the system made it as imperceptible to users as the beating of their own hearts, so that the attention of revolutionaries came to be focused anywhere but on the notation. 'Notational reform' was left to the theorists – watchers on the sidelines, whose suggestions never had the least influence on the general musical situation.

Today, all this is changed. Current philosophical trends, the new and expanding communication sciences, the need to discover how best we can talk to the machines which play an increasing part in our lives – all tend to focus attention on the process of communication itself, as something that can be manipulated to our advantage or disadvantage. Musicians have woken up to the significance of the notational link, and the possibility of acting on the whole complex of musical activities through the notation. There is a reversal of the traditional position, in which the notation is thought of as existing for the sake of the music. As Kagel says, 'the relationship is the other way round today; the development of particular notations implies a latent development in the musical language'.[66] Only the traditionalists among today's composers accept the system as it stands. For the advanced composer there is, it seems, what amounts to a moral obligation to reconsider; to add new symbols to those already in existence, or to set up new playing and listening situations by devising new notational methods of appeal. The interest of many new works is often centred on the originality, even beauty, of the notation. Reviews of new music will give up most of their space to detailed accounts of notational innovations. Players are coming to accept the prospect of 'tackling a new set of rules and symbols every time they approach a new composition'. David Behrman goes on to say that learning a new piece can be 'like learning a new game or a new grammar, and first rehearsals are often taken up by a discussion of the rules about "how" to play rather than "how well" '.[67] Even though the great mass of practical music-making still goes on in the same old way, unaffected by innovation, notational reform has at last passed out of the stage of theory into a stage of practical application.

In talking about modern experimental notations, we can no longer attempt to relate all innovations to a central system, or try to list all the custom-built symbols that composers invent for their private purposes. Many of the innovations imply a total upset of the old composer-performer relationship; and the speed of development is so great that any comprehensive list of symbols would be outdated long before it was finished. All we can hope to do is to suggest a classification that reflects current aims and preoccupations, illustrated with a few sample extracts that show symbols and systems in use.

Minor innovations within the system
Simplifications, rationalizations, and refinements may be made within the system; in many cases, the writer's interest may be only to find a clearer way of writing, and no new musical situation may be envisaged. The novelty lies in the fact that such innovations are now introduced by working composers, and that players are therefore forced to come to terms with the new symbols or methods if they want to play the works in which they are used. Many examples have been given in earlier chapters of this type of innovation: Stravinsky's accent marks, Britten's curlew sign, Stockhausen's use of the sharp as the sole accidental, and his sforzando accent notation could be mentioned once more. Often such signs may have little practical purpose, and we may suspect that they

are introduced, rather as a new type face is introduced by a magazine layout man, to give the music an interesting, up-to-date look – and, after all, why not? Connolly's accelerandi built into the beams, many of the picturesque time signatures of contemporary scores can be read as a declaration of an advanced, forward-looking attitude and no more. The current vogue for pictorial symbols, in road signs, timetables, catalogues, and directories is also reflected in notation (see below). In practice, it often takes far longer to look up the symbols in the index than to read a verbal instruction.

In some cases, however, modifications are both simple and purposeful. From the convoluted conventional notations of the

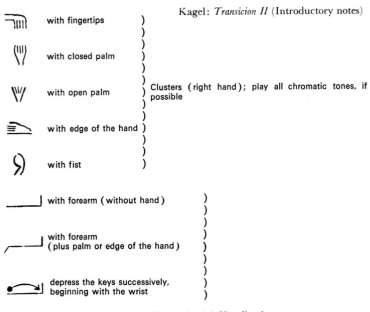

Kagel: *Transicion II* (Introductory notes)

⊐⫿⫿⫿	with fingertips	)
		)
		)
(⫿⫿⫿)	with closed palm	)
		)
		)
\⫿⫿/	with open palm	) Clusters (right hand); play all chromatic tones, if possible
		)
⫥⫥	with edge of the hand	)
		)
		)
ϟ)	with fist	)

_____⌐	with forearm (without hand)	)
		)
		)
⌐‾‾‾⌐	with forearm (plus palm or edge of the hand)	)
		)
		)
		)
●━━━⌐	depress the keys successively, beginning with the wrist	)

From the AA Handbook.

✕	Restaurant classification (see page 23)
⚹	Country-house hotel
⌄	Garage classification (see page 13)
▶◀	Breakdown service normally available 24 hours every day unless otherwise shown
⋈◯	Breakdown service normally available Monday/Friday (unless otherwise stated) until hours shown
▪	Petrol and oil available to midnight or later where shown

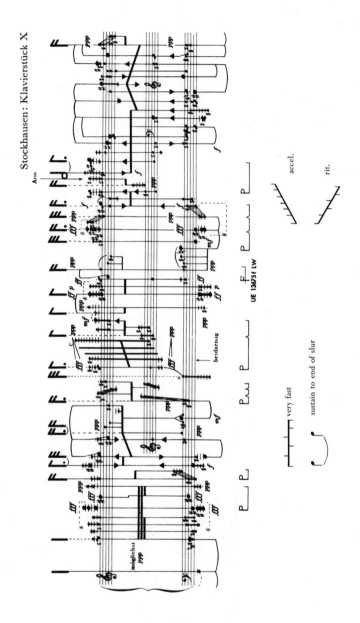

Stockhausen: Klavierstück X

UE 13675 f LW

134

earlier piano pieces, Stockhausen advanced to the simplified *Klavierstück X* (see previous page), devoid of meaninglessly precise specification, and using new symbolization elegantly and clearly within a conventional framework.

Notations that involve extension of techniques

The prototype of this group is Cowell's note cluster symbolization, which also illustrates the way in which a new activity and a new notation can develop in partnership. The cluster symbol appears to be no more than a simplification of the possible but complicated notation of 'all notes between x and y'; yet it was from the first associated with experimental techniques, such as the special wooden boards with which Cowell's clusters were to be played; while the notation itself has surely been part-inspirer of such later developments as the glissando clusters of Penderecki (p. 52). The ease with which a new notation can be adapted to some purposes but not to others can be a directing factor in an experimental situation.

The examples given in the section on timbre (p. 80) illustrated another characteristic of experimental notations – that they are often concerned with action rather than sounds. This is always likely to be so, since any new sound implies a new method of sound production, and therefore puts us back into a teaching situation – the player needs to be taught what should be done, before he can produce the required sound. But it is also a part of the mystique of many experimental notators that they should be more concerned with a player's actions than with the sounds produced. 'Let the notations refer to what is to be done, not what is to be heard' Cage has written; while Cardew's 'A notation should be directed to a large extent towards the people who read it rather than towards the sounds they will make' displays the same tendency to think of the sound as a by-product of the activity, which is therefore specified exactly while the sound may be left to look after itself.

As we have seen, it is not unusual to find seating plans or instrument arrangement plans included in the score for the convenience of the performers, and to ensure coordination. Today, and particularly in electronic music, the direction from which sounds reach the listener can be part of the structure of the music, and is duly noted in the score. An extreme form of space notation is found in Cardew's *Four Pieces* (on the following page), in which the position alone of the sound event is notated:

135

●   Sounds made at floor level
○   Sounds made above floor level
◐   Sounds both on and above floor level

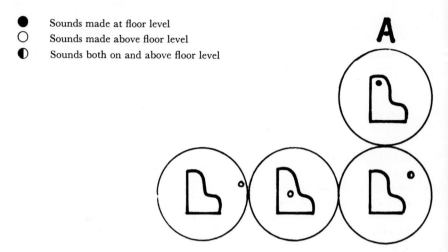

A

The notation refers to any sound events caused in the neighbourhood of the grand piano.

With the extension of the boundaries to include actions and phenomena never before accepted as belonging to 'music', notation too has to extend its range in unforeseen directions:

.30

Cage: Water Music

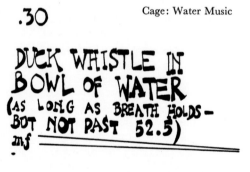

DUCK WHISTLE IN BOWL OF WATER (AS LONG AS BREATH HOLDS— BUT NOT PAST 52.5) mf

Cage: Changes

Upper figures give wavelengths to which radio is tuned.
Lower figures give dynamics.

Cage: Water Music

5·4525
Pour water from
one receptacle
to another

5·5025

ff

Pour water

136

New systems

No new universal notation has appeared that can be appropriately used for all types of music. Equiton and Klavarscribo, the two most widely discussed new systems, offer too few advantages to the traditionalists, and are too rigid to attract the avant-garde. Klavarscribo is firmly linked to the piano keyboard; neither offers provision for the relaxations or refinements of pitch control with which experimental writers are so often concerned. Both systems, however, adopt proportional time notation, the most important innovation of our time, and the only one to have established its usefulness in many different contexts. It seems unlikely that proportionate notation, in spite of its attractive simplicity, will ever supersede conventional notation in music of regular metric structure. Its measured lengths do not represent the way in which we sense time intervals in metric music, in which measurement by reference to the beating of our own internal clock remains the most accurate method.* The situation has been confused because proportionate notations do indeed give exact, high-definition specifications – but not in terms we can easily interpret. In practice, their effective use (and that of all the other newly devised notations now to be mentioned), is closely bound up with the creation of new playing situations. Proportionate notations are significant largely for the fact that they force us to sense the passage of time in a new way: they represent, in fact, the thin end of the wedge of indeterminacy. It is from the idea of indeterminacy that many of the most interesting new notational ideas of the moment spring; the confusing variety of systems and philosophies involved can at any rate be related back to a single central point.

Indeterminate notations

All notations are indeterminate in so far as they fail to give a complete specification. Conventional notation is indeterminate in matters of pitch, timbre, method of attack. Figured-bass notation leaves the details of realization to the performer; the 6 under a note says, in effect, 'any sixth (and third, and octave) appropriate to the context'. Schoenberg's ✗ says, in effect, 'somewhere round about this pitch'. In all but the extremer forms of indeterminacy, what really happens is that there is a switch of attention. Where

* The *only* case of exact correspondence between sensory data and external phenomena is in perception of time-succession – all other impressions are symbolic.' M. Helmholtz.[68]

we were once exclusively concerned with the pitch, durations, and ordering of notes, we are now prepared to leave these matters to the discretion of the player (as we once did the dynamics and timbre), or to single out one aspect only of the music for precise definition.

The least extreme forms of indeterminacy are found in such works as Boulez's *Pli selon Pli* and Stockhausen's *Klavierstück XI*. Here, the notational problems are mainly those of layout, and much ingenuity has gone to the presentation of material in forms where orders can be systematically or spontaneously varied. All the alternatives may appear on one immense page (2′ by 1′ 3″ for Boulez's *Piano Sonata no. 3*, 3′ by 1′ 9″ for Stockhausen's *Klavierstück XI*). Single pages, which may be arranged in any order, may contain cut-out windows that frame fragments from the underlying page as in Pousseur's *Caractères*. Stockhausen's *Zyklus* is issued in loose leaf format, so that the work may start at any point on any page, and be played round till the same point is reached again. The score may be used either way up, and many alternatives are provided, parallel passages appearing in brackets or within triangles meeting at an apex:

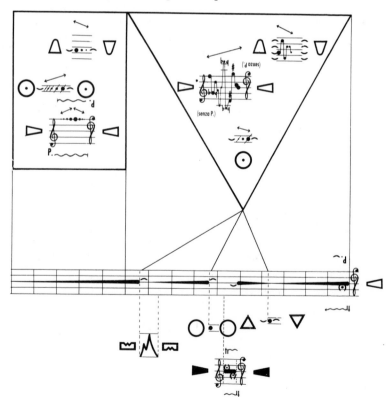

Another possibility is for the performing material (fully composed or indeterminate) to appear within squares or frames, with instructions for determining an order of performance, as in Haubenstock-Ramati's *Credentials*:

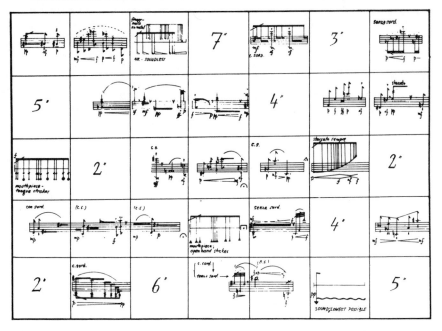

Scores may also offer alternatives in matters of detail as well as in the ordering of sections. Stockhausen's *Mixtur* allows a player to choose any ten notes out of a section for special accentuation; Boulez's *Eclat* offers a choice of alternative dynamic schemes; Cage in his *Solo for Voice* and *Concert for Piano and Orchestra* uses notes of various sizes which may be read as specifying differences of either amplitude or duration at the player's choice. Going one stage further, we can be told to 'perform within a specified range' as in:

Kagel: Transicion II

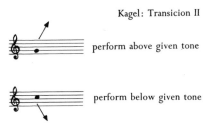

or to play any note within a high, medium, or low register (see p. 56). Graphical notations may give an approximate indication of pitch, in which the detailed execution is left to the performer (see p. 56). Kagel's *Transicion II* provides material which may, but need not, be used on supplementary systems; or notes may appear on discs, which can be rotated so that when they are read vertically, different sets of notes appear in combination. Stockhausen's *Refrain* uses curved staves on a single stiff card, with a swivelling transparent plastic rule that can be variously positioned to decide the exact form of a single performance.

A bizarre form of indeterminacy is brought about by the creation of deliberately paradoxical situations, in which the apparently specific instructions *cannot* be executed according to the directive. In Christian Wolff's *6 players* the viola is told to play eight notes in a quarter of a second, including three harmonics and one pizzicato. In this impossible situation, the player finds what solution he can – he might, for instance, so Cardew suggests, play as many as he can in the time, then distribute the remainder over the whole of the rest of the piece. . . . (In Cardew's own *Four Pieces* this instruction is given: 'Ignore any two of the indications for any particular beat; if the remaining indications are considered in any respect mutually exclusive, play nothing.')

Notation as source material or rulebook

The simplest forms of indeterminacy so far discussed have often involved no more than a shuffling of sections – no deeper principle may be involved than permission to vary the order of items in a concert programme. In more extreme cases, the performer is allowed further into the compositional game, and the score ceases to be a directive to be acted on immediately, becoming instead a source book or rule book. Wolff's *For six players* and Stockhausen's *Plus Minus* (to take two examples of many available) are really 'do it yourself' composing kits. They contain a number of separate sets of basic notations, with instructions explaining how material may be selected and developed from these source-groups to build up a performable work. The idea of a notation that can be read directly, either quickly or laboriously, has been left behind. Such works often demand the preparation of a secondary score, in which the performer works out his own version of the basic material.

The score may also be thought of as a set of rules for a new type of musical game, together with the necessary material for playing.

Lukas Foss describes the basic idea of *Echoi IV* thus: 'Jump back and forth between different spots in the music at the crack of a "whip" – wrong sound anvil struck at the whim of a percussionist . . . the music is slapped back and forth in time.'[69] (Foss finds a similarity between this game and the false starts in the trio of Beethoven's Fifth Symphony.) Feldman's *Duration I* looks, in score, like an atonal chorale, with long rows of crotchets for each player. Here, the rules are simple: start together; move independently, each player deciding for himself on the duration of each note; stop when you reach the finishing line. The slowest player will be left stranded, the shelter of his companions' sounds removed. Christian Wolff's *Duet II* for horn and piano is a more complicated game. The rule-symbols and a sample passage are given on the following page. Some of the procedures are described by David Behrman: 'To begin, and every time a fragment has been completed, the first player to make the next sound determines which fragment is to come next by playing the first sound of that fragment. The other player hears the sound, recognizes the fragment that it begins, and responds by playing his own part in that fragment. Or, he may a) fail to recognize the cue, b) start another fragment himself simultaneously with the first player. In any case, the directions provide that as soon as the players realize that they are not playing the same fragment together, they should break off and "start" all over again. . . .

'During the fragments themselves . . . the time at which a player begins or ends his next sound may be determined by him or by a sound made by the other player. In the latter event, he must wait for the other's sound to occur and then react to it – sometimes as fast as he can – without the benefit of advance warning. . . . Here the player's situation might be compared to that of a ping-pong player awaiting his opponent's fast serve: he knows what is coming (the serve) and knows what he must do when it comes (return it); but the details of how and when these things take place are determined only at the moment of their occurrence.'[67]

Stockhausen's *Intervall* (first performed in May 1972) consists of 'rules' without playing material. The work is for two players at one piano, and the directive begins: 'Play single notes with irregular time-intervals and dynamics. Every time that one of your attacks coincides with an attack from the other player, add a note, till you play in 10-note chords. . . .'

In these musical games, we cannot expect to see the 'interest' of

141

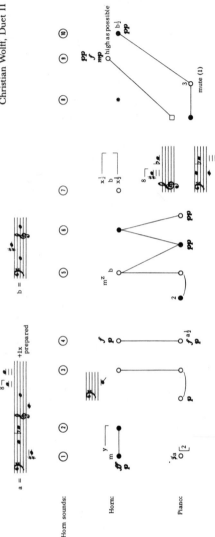

Horn sounds:

① ② ③ ④ ⑤ ⑥ ⑦ ⑧ ⑨ ⑩

Horn:

Piano:

♭ = line means 1) notes must be unequal in some respect (e.g. duration or loudness); 2) notes must be varied each time the section is repeated.

[2 = 2 notes are to be attacked simultaneously.

a♩ b♩ = transpose any of the tones in the source half a tone higher or lower.

b⌐x♯⌐ = raise or lower pitches (of source b) half a tone and transpose to any higher octave.

m^y and m² = two different kinds of mutes or muting (to be chosen by player).

(Duration: ● = 1 second or less; ○ = any; □ = very long to medium.

* = a noise

3   play 3 notes of any duration,
0   together, overlapping, or
     separate. Silence
     between tones is free. Mute one
     of them.

H (Horn player)   start and stop together

P (Pianist)

P starts, holds till H sounds; both release together

P plays (short note). H begins short note as P's note ends.

H plays short note. P starts at its end, holds any duration.

mute (1)

high as possible

a particular game foreshadowed in the score; nor is there any guarantee that the most interesting games to play will produce interesting results for listeners. Behrman does indeed describe appreciatively 'the thin sustaining sound made by a player who is waiting for his cue and is not sure if he has missed it'; but the point of the activity lies in the activity itself.

Implicit notations
The unsatisfactorily named implicit notations provide a stimulus for the performer in which no defined end-result or type of activity is foreseeable. The symbol is a starting-point for musical activity, and is designed to encourage a personal response. This family of signs is often enigmatic or paradoxical: its members may or may not be related to the conventional signs of notation. These signs may stand on their own as objects of visual appeal, and they are designed, not to make objective, referential statements, but to stimulate the performer to action, appealing to him in terms of his own intellectual and aesthetic association patterns. So we arrive at the point where Cornelius Cardew can write 'the only criterion for a sound is – was the player expecting to make it?'[35]

Robert Moran: Four Visions, no. 2

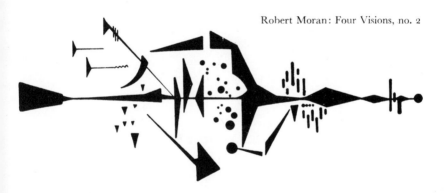

For flute, harp, and string quartet. Duration, from 1' 15 to 1' 35. Some of the symbols are explained in the foreword; the inverted triangle signifies 'Strong entry, pizzicato, strong pizzicato with string rebounding against fingerboard, additional noise on body of instrument'. No detailed instructions for realization are given.

143

For voices. Sloping of staves indicates accelerando or ritenuto.
Dotted lines indicate points of synchronization.

Cardew has given examples of ways in which his signs in *Octet '61* might be translated in performance:

Cornelius Cardew: Octet '61

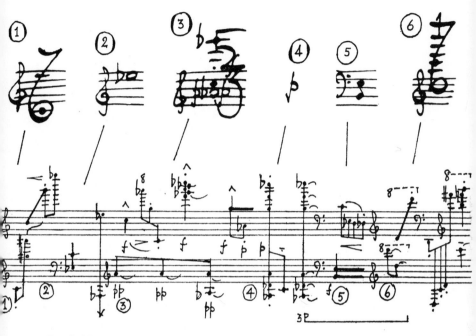

Partial key to example above:

1. Seven taken literally as a configuration in musical space. Six Cs, one added to each of the first six signs
2. Add E flats
3. Three As. Five A flats. Three sustained notes *forte*: the others *piano* or *pianissimo*. Five-note cluster-type chord
4. Two chords *piano* following the dot-dash rhythm of the Gs in 3
5. Slide from E down towards B
6. Six different registers for D (colour pitch). Seven described as in 1. One described as subsequent cluster. One C at given pitch – longer duration

Where all responsibility is thrown onto the performer, 'inspirational' might be an apter description than 'implicit'. In Cardew's *Treatise*, no instructions at all are given as to the order in which pages are to be taken, the instruments to be used, or the degree of

145

consistency to be aimed at in reacting to recurring symbols. 'There's a master plan for this piece which determines where certain elements are going to preponderate' Cardew tells us; Roger Smalley, reviewing the work, can refer to 'the almost Webernian precision of pp. 46/47'.[70]

Cardew: Treatise, pp. 46–47

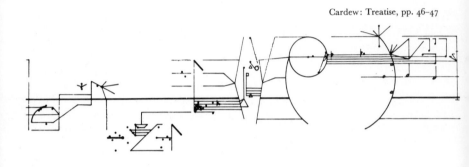

Yet the freedom granted to the performer is absolute; there can be no objective standard by which to compare performances. At this point, notation ceases to have any resemblance to a language in the common sense of the word. There are no referents, there is no prior agreement between users as to the meaning of any sign. Should we think of these scores as instruction books or as works of art? Perhaps as both – Earle Brown's scores have in fact been exhibited at art galleries, while the Japanese composer Takemitsu has collaborated with the designer Kohei Sugiura to produce score-pictures that may be either played or exhibited. Conversely, the initiative may come from the artist; Malcolm Carder's abstracts are produced to be looked at, but may also be performed.

In like manner, Xenakis has produced a score which is both a directive for musical performance and an architectural design – an exhibition pavilion for the Brussels World Fair of 1958, and the music to be played within it.

Why this sudden and overwhelming interest in notational experiment, at this particular moment in musical history? Why indeterminism? Why the flight from the single, universal notation that has served us so long? There is, of course, no single answer; but several contributing causes can be named.

1) The avant-garde composer, generally weakly placed to exercise economic pressure, must win the performer to his side if he is to get performances. Indeterminate notations seek, by involving the performer more deeply in the creative activity, to enlist him as collaborator rather than employee.

2) The switching of interest from pitch-time relationships forces a reconstruction of the notational system, which conventionally says to us 'play the right notes (right in pitch and time); take your own decisions about dynamics, articulation, balance. . . .'

3) In an age when developments in communications are transforming our lives, attention is focused on the media of communication. Simultaneous or haphazard methods of presentation, and variable order patterns, reflect our dissatisfaction with the rigid linear ordering of material imposed for so long by the conventions of the printed page.

4) The need for a universal language was greatest when music was re-created from the written note for each performance, and when a mass of literate amateurs could make direct contact with the composer via the score. Today, with the help of record, radio, and television, a composer's reputation can be established by the performances of a few initiates – even by a single recording of a unique performance. The private language is no longer, necessarily, a bar to dissemination.

5) The original function of notation – to preserve for posterity – has today been taken over by the recording. Notation is therefore set free to assume any form, no longer needing to foreshadow the end-result (in some cases, however, new scores include a recording in a pocket at the back, so that we are given both specification and description of the finished work).

147

6) The private language protects the work against non-understanding performers: Cardew, in the preface to his *Four Works*, writes: 'Pieces need camouflage to protect them from hostile forces in the early days of their life. One kind of protection is provided by the novelty and uniqueness of the notation; few musicians will take the trouble to decipher and learn the notations unless they have a positive interest in performing the works'.*

7) Photographic processes and technical developments in book-production have made possible experiments in layout and format that would have been impracticable in earlier ages.

* Secret notations are nothing new. Morley wrote: 'The French who were generally accounted great masters, seldom or never would prick their lessons as they played them, much less reveal anything in the thorough understanding of the instrument.'[71]

18 *Where Now?*

From one point of view, today's revolutionary notations can be thought of as anti-notations, both in general and specific senses. They seek to undermine the traditional composer-performer relationship: they imply that the old tools of the trade are obsolete. The most extreme *implicit* graphical notations, in refusing to do more than inspire the performer in the most general sense, suggest that the whole idea of musical literacy is due for abandonment.

Objections to Musical Literacy, in general, can be convincingly argued. No one can deny that a fully literate society creates for itself certain problems and risks. Every advantage offered by the use of a fully-notated music carries with it an attendant disadvantage:

1) Notation preserves (thereby creating population problems: what happens when old works never die?).

2) Notation creates a new role for the composer, that of 'specialist in musical substance' (and reduces the status, responsibilities, and perhaps capacities of the executant,* at the same time isolating the creator so that he is insulated from the vital act of realization).

3) Notation makes possible a calculated music (creating a double set of sometimes conflicting values in eye and ear musics).

4) Notation regularizes and orders what was previously vague and uncertain (and in so doing, reduces our idea of music to 'that which can be notated';† that is, we make the meanings

---

* See Thamus's reply to Theuth, the inventor of letters, as recounted by Socrates: 'This discovery of yours will create forgetfulness in the learner's souls, because they will not use their memories; they will trust to the external written characters and not remember of themselves. The specific which you have discovered is an aid not to memory but to recollection, and you give your disciples only the semblance of truth; they will hear much and learn nothing; they will appear to know much and will generally know nothing; they will be tiresome company, for they will seem wise without being wise.'[72]

† 'Permeation of colloquial language with literate uniform qualities has flattened out educated speech till it is a very reasonable acoustic facsimile of the uniform and continuous visual effects of typography.'[18]

of our music from the notateable sounds, as we choose fruits for tinning by selecting those which will survive the tinning process – so, split or bent notes appear as rarely on the daily menu as mangoes).

5) Notation makes possible a methodical, step-by-step, description of sound-events (or alternatively, replaces a meaningful ful continuity by a meaningless particularity).

There is, of course, no going back from literacy. All those who question the assumptions and standards of a literate society themselves use the letters, words, communication techniques whose uses they deplore. It seems to be invariably the highly literate who protest most strongly against the tyrant who rules them; avant-garde notations are the exercises and diversions of highly educated, literate, musicians. Experimenters can launch their whole-hearted attacks against the walls, secure in the knowledge that these walls will not suddenly crumble into dust. The great mass of the world's musical business is certain to be transacted, for a long time to come, in some variant of conventional notation as we know it today; just as the world's practical affairs will be discussed, written about, and transacted in the common language of the day.

Something should be said in defence of conventional, gradually-developed languages, which have certain great advantages to offer as compared with the artificial codes of the new-language-makers. In the first place, their stiff and pedantic characters are more apparent than real. For the child, spelling out his first reading book or learning his first piano piece, the written language does indeed speak in a governess-y tone of voice, doling out the meaning in arbitrary units that seem to deny the fluid, connected performance that we think of as intelligent or musical. It is the fuller knowledge, accumulated by long experience, of musical situations and of the conventional representations of them that renders notation effective. As James said, the true reading comes out of the reader's mind rather than out of the symbols themselves. Languages acquire depth, as users acquire the background knowledge of possible connotations that gives to every combination of symbols, in every context, its own subtly shaded inflection of meaning. It is this depth of meaning that the codes, the artificial languages of avant-garde notations, inevitably lack. I would even suggest that where experimental notations are used with success they are often successful because they release the potential of performers whose sensitivity and insight has been developed by long, conventional training, so that the performance is a result of previous discipline and present liberation. Lastly, in defence of conventional notations, it should be said that two of the most commonly-made assumptions of notation reformers are of doubtful validity. First, that direct graphical appeal to the eye is an essential feature of a truthful notation.* Second, that simplification and rationalization will necessarily produce better results. Most notations and languages serve their users effectively on a nongraphical symbolic basis; many languages (including English and French) are full of inconsistencies and complexities that make the language harder to learn, but have no effect on the efficiency of the system once they are mastered.

McLuhan has pointed out how long it takes us to come to terms with a new communication medium. The telegraph was first used for betting and long distance chess, Telstar for sausage eating contests. In the excitement of discovery, we enjoy and wonder at new techniques for their own sakes: what we do with them counts for less than the fact of their existence. This is the situation that has arisen twice in the history of Western music; in the late fourteenth century, when the development of mensural notations led to the complexities of the first wholly-calculated music; and in our own day, when we have once more woken up to the fact that a notation is not a part of the inevitable order, but is a tool that we ourselves can modify, replace, and develop in any one of many directions. Then, as now, a huge variety of notations came into being. Then as now, the mechanism of notation fascinated its users, who could be more interested in the working of the system than in the end-results of the process.

Two influential trends of thought that seem certain to affect the nature of Western music and its notations for many years to come deserve special mention. From the avant-garde, comes the idea that notation can evolve in the direction of freedom as well as in the direction of greater control. This development was foreshadowed in the harmonic advances of the early twentieth century, where situations were thrown up in which the running of parts to exact timetables was no longer a strict necessity. It was the necessity of avoiding discord that made exact synchronization into a vital organizing principle. (In the same way, trains have to run to a timetable partly because they must not be

* Thus, Karkoshka, in his book on new notations,[73] declares that an essential requirement of any reformed notation is that signs must develop from the visual sense – be psycho-visually 'correct'.

151

allowed to collide. Make trains of soft rubber, and the timetables can be relaxed.) From ethnomusicology and electronic music has come the idea that other characteristics of sound beside pitch and duration can be meaningfully and exactly used in making music. These are, surely, two main motivating forces behind the most startling new developments of our day.

Can we ever hope to move back towards a single notation, to serve popular and esoteric uses? At present, when the more extreme notators parade their nonconformity and reject all conventional symbols as resolutely as Schoenberg rejected the major triad, the possibility seems remote. Who is to define terms acceptable to all? Who is to control uses of symbols that depart from official interpretations? When notational attitudes as diverse and extreme as Boulez's and Cage's exist at the same moment, how can a common language evolve to serve all purposes? It seems certain that we can expect a long period during which traditional and specialist notations will coexist, with (one hopes) fruitful cross-influence. If fusion ever takes place between seeming incompatibles, it will occur, not as the result of the activities of inventive notational reformers, but because musicians of all cultures (pop, classical, and avant-garde, or their successors) once more want to perform together in closely-coordinated consort.

Postscript

'Reread the first page of these pensées and you will see that it has become quite mouldy' Stravinsky wrote in his *Dialogues and a Diary*. Since I began this book, there have been many new developments in the notation situation. Cardew has publicly repudiated the underlying ethics of his *Treatise* (see p. 146). At an International Symposium on the problems of graphic music held at Rome in October 1972*, Kurt Stone outlined proposals for a handbook to codify the meanings of all symbols now currently in use, and E. Karkoshka was still exploring the possibilities of an expanded traditional notation; but many composers were claiming that music had already passed the point where notation was even relevant.

In pop groups and among experimental composers, the tape recorder is increasingly used as a composing tool by means of which the inspiration of the moment may be fixed, considered, worked over at leisure; the first 'Use' of a written notation suggested on p. 9 is thus largely taken over by the recorder. In another field, too, the record is taking over; today, bandleaders rarely make use of piano–conductor scores (see p. 7), preferring to work direct from recordings. Meanwhile, some of Cage's recent scores—meticulously disposed assemblies of letters and symbols made up of hundreds of different sorts of letraset—can be read as exercises in abstract score-making; realization in sound being almost irrelevant to what is already a finished work of art.

Many composers are using, with increasing effectiveness, notations that combine conventional (determinate) and indeterminate elements; admirable examples can be found in the recent scores of Lutoslawski. In the last few years, though interest in indeterminate and improvisatory music has certainly not decreased, less attention has been focused on notational innovation for its own sake. Many of the wilder notational experiments of the past decades will no doubt soon be forgotten, and there is some reason to hope that, when all is done, we shall be left with a wider and more versatile vocabulary of directive signs than at any previous time in the history of Western Music.

July 1973

* Reported by Colin Brumby, *Musical Times*, January 1973.

List of Sources

		Page
1	W. Kaufman, *Musical Notations of the Orient*, Indiana UP, 1967	6, 7, 42
2	E. Wellesz, *Byzantine Music and Hymnography*, OUP, 1961	7
3	R. H. van Gulik, *Lore of the Chinese Lute*, Tokyo, 1940	12
4	Colin Cherry, Lecture at the Institute of Contemporary Arts (17 February 1970)	12
*5	Simeon Potter, *Our Language*, Pelican, 1950	12
*6	Thurston Dart, *The Interpretation of Music*, Hutchinson's UL, 1954	14, 57, 127
7	John Parry, *Psychology of Human Communication*, ULP, London, 1967	14
8	E. H. Gombrich, *Meditations on a Hobby Horse and other essays on the theory of art*, Phaidon, 1963	14
9	T. C. Grame, *Musicology and Performance*, *J. Eth.* vii, February 1963	15
10	Arthur Honegger, quoted in *The world of the virtuoso* by Marc Pincherle, Gollancz, 1964	18, 130
*11	Colin Mares, *Communication*, English Universities Press, 1966	21
*12	Colin Cherry, *On Human Communication*, MIT Press,	22
13	E. B. Huey, *Psychology and Pedagogy of Reading*, New York, 1910	23
14	William James, *Principles of Psychology*, Macmillan, 1890	23
15	Axel Wijk, Paper in *Acta Universitas Stolkholmiensis*, quoted in *Fundamentals of Speech* by George Hibbitt, Doubleday, NY, 1962	28
16	Charles Burney, *General History of Music*, London, 1789	31-32
17	D'Arcy Thompson, *On the Nature and Action of Certain Ligaments* (1894) quoted in *The Art of the Soluble* by P. B. Medawar, Methuen, 1967	36
18	Marshall Macluhan, *Understanding Media*, Routledge and Kegan Paul, 1964	36, 150
19	James Mainwaring, article on *Gestalt* in Grove's Dictionary of Music, 5th edition, Macmillan, 1954	36
20	C. Sachs, *The Rise of Music in the Ancient World*, London, 1944	37
21	J. McLeod, *Composer* 13, Winter, 1965	42
22	E. Ghent, *Programmed signals to performers*, Perspectives of New Music, Fall–Winter 1967	42

<table>
<tr><td></td><td></td><td align="right">*Page*</td></tr>
</table>

23 K. Stockhausen, talk at St. John's, Smith Square, London, 10 January 1970 — 43

24 J. Wolf, *Handbuch der Notationskunde*, Leipzig, 1913 — 48

25 Charles Ives, early draft of *Some Quarter-tone Impressions* quoted by Howard Boatwright, PNM, Spring–Summer 1965 — 50

26 Henry Cowell, *Current Chronicle*, MQ, January 1952 — 56

27 Curt Sachs, *Rhythm and Tempo*, Dent, 1953 — 57

28 W. Apel, *The Notation of Polyphonic Music*, Cambridge, Mass., 1953 — 57

29 Arthur Jacobs, letter to the *Musical Times*, August 1969 — 59

30 Yfrah Neaman and Howard Ferguson in *Composer*, 1967 — 62

31 Christopher Simpson, *The Principles of Practical Musick*, London, 1665 — 68

32 Richard Wagner, *Prose Works*, vol. IV, tr. W. A. Ellis, Kegan Paul, 1895 — 68

*33 Kurt Stone, *Some problems and methods of Notation*, PNM, Spring 1963 — 71

34 A. L. Lloyd, *The sensation of loudness*, Music and Letters, July 1953 — 74

*35 Cornelius Cardew, *Notation-Interpretation, etc.* Tempo, Summer 1961 — 75, 125, 144

36 B. Bartolozzi, *New Sounds for Woodwind*, OUP, 1969 — 77

37 Mantle Hood, *The challenge of Bi-musicality*, *J. Eth.* iv, 1960 — 78

*38 Bruno Nettl, *Theory and Method in Ethnomusicology*, NY Free Press of Glencoe, 1964 — 79

*39 Gardner Read, *Notation*, Allyn and Bacon, Boston, 1964 — 84, 130

*40 H. Keller, *Phrasing and Articulation*, Barrie and Rockliff, 1966 — 85

41 H. Schenker, preface to last Beethoven piano sonatas (UE) — 87

*42 Donald Martino, *Notation in general—articulation in particular*, PNM, Spring 1966 — 89

43 Rudolf Reti, *Thematic Process in Music*, Faber, 1961 — 98

44 L. Salzer, *Structural Hearing*, Ch. Coni, N.Y, 1952 — 98

45 Brian Dennis, *Experimental Music in Schools*, OUP, 1969 — 103

46 B. L. Whorf, *Language, Thought and Reality*, Tech. Review, London, 1939 — 105

*47 Bartók and Lord, *Serbo-Croatian Folk Songs*, Columbia UP, NY, 1955 — 105

48 E. von Hornbostel, 'The music of the Fuegians', Ethnos, 1961 (quoted in Kolinski's *Recent trends in Ethnomusicology*, *J.Eth.* xi, January 1967) — 107

*49 I. Bengtsson, *On melody registration and 'Mona' in Elektronische Datenverabeitung in der Musikwissenschaft*, Bosse, Regensburg, 1967   110, 111
50 J. Blacking, *Problems of pitch, pattern and harmony in the Ocarina music of the Venda*, African Music 2, Roodeport, 1955   111
51 C. Seeger, *Toward a universal sound-writing for musicology*, J. of Int. Folk Music Council 9, 1957   111
52 I. Stravinsky, *Conversations with I.S.*, Faber and Faber, 1959   112, 127
53 P. Zinovieff, Programme note for concert at Queen Elizabeth Hall, London, 15 January 1968   113, 121
54 B. S. Brook and Murray Gould, article in *Fontes Artes Musicae* XI, 1964   118
55 Mathews and Rosler in *Music by Computers*, ed. Foerster and Beauchamp, John Wiley and Sons, 1969   121
56 Ernest Newman, *More essays from the World of Music*, Calder, 1958   122
57 Vernon Lee, *Music and its Lovers*, Allen and Unwin, 1932   122
58 Ernest Fowles, *Eye and Hand in harmony study*, OUP, 1932   122
59 Aaron Copland, *Music and Imagination*, Mentor books, 1959 (originally Harvard UP, 1952)   123
60 Charles Ives, from 'Catalogue of unpublished works' *Charles Ives and his music* by Henry and Sidney Cowell, OUP, 1955 (not in later edition)   125
61 Schoenberg, *Letters*, Faber and Faber, 1964   127
*62 Lukas Foss, *The Changing Composer-Performer Relationship*, PNM, Spring 1963   128, 129
63 Ernst Krenek, *Music Here and Now*, Russell, NY, 1967   129
64 C. H. Kitson, *Rudiments of Music*, OUP, 1957   130
65 R. Gerhard, in *Notations* (John Cage), Something Else Press, NY, 1969   130
66 M. Kagel, Translation-Rotation, *Die Reihe* no. 7, 1965   132
67 D. Behrman, *What indeterminate notation determines*, PNM, Spring–Summer 1965   132, 141
68 H. Helmholtz, *On the Sensations of Tone*, tr. A. J. Ellis, Dover, NY, 1954   137
69 L. Foss, *Work Notes for Echoi*, PNM, Fall–Winter 1964   141
70 R. Smalley, *Musical Times*, May 1968   146
71 T. Morley, quoted in *The Story of Notation* (Abdy Williams), Walter Scott Publishing Co., 1903   148
72 Plato, *Phaedrus*, tr. B. Jowett, OUP, 1871   149
73 E. Karkoshka, *Das Schriftbild des Neuen Musik*, Moeck, Celle, 1966. English edition, UE, 1972   151

For further reading

Books starred in the List of Sources are recommended for further reading: Potter (5) and Mares (11) as concise guides to languages and communication studies, Cherry (4) for those who want to investigate more deeply. Dart (6) offers practical information on the interpretation of music from 12th to 18th centuries (nothing on more recent periods). Read (39) is a comprehensive guide to conventional notations in present use. Keller (40) covers the evolution of phrasing and articulation up to the end of the nineteenth century, but not beyond. The preface to *Serbo-Croatian Folk Songs* (47) discusses the practical problems facing the collector when he comes to notate the music he has collected, and Nettl (37) deals with wider aspects of ethnomusicologists' notations. Seeger's article on Descriptive and Prescriptive notations in the *Musical Quarterly*, 1944, is well worth reading for its broad view of notational questions. Bengtsson (49) is interesting on the distinctions between physical, perceived, and notated sound-events, and for his formulation of general principles for the notation of folk musics. The many articles on notation in *Perspectives of New Music* (including some not mentioned here) have formed part of a continuing *Notation Forum*. Together with Cardew's *Tempo* article (35) they offer a stimulating commentary on developing avant-garde attitudes. Karkoshka (73) has many examples of experimental notations; and, for those who read German, the Notation number of *Darmstädter Beiträge zur neuen Musik*, vol. IX (Schott) is also recommended. Apel's *Harvard Dictionary of Music* (Heinemann), with an excellent cross-reference system, is very useful for concise information on early notations, and Archibald Jacob's *Musical Handwriting* (OUP) is excellent for all practical problems of manuscript writing, part-copying, and lay-out.

Index

Accelerando   13, 72, 73, 134
Action notation   6, 38, 40, 41, 79, 135
Ambiguity   14, 33, 85, 130
Arditi   **66**

Bach, Johann Sebastian   99
Baritone-Martin   78
Bartók, Béla   17, 40, 50, 52, 65, 69, 79, 82, **84**, **88**, 105, **106**, 107
Bartolozzi, Bruno   **77**, 79
Beaming   86-9;   secondary uses   71, 73, 77, 79
Bedford, David   69, 80
Beethoven, Ludwig van   28, 30, 31, 51, **75**, 82, **85**, **86**, 94, 141
Behrman, David   132, 141, 143
Bengtsson, Ingmar   109, 111
Berg, Alban   **54**, 94, 96
Berio, Luçiano   **68**, 72
Berlioz, Hector   83, **85**
Blacking, J.   111 n.
Blaukopf, Kurt   32 n.
Borodin, Alexander•   31
Boulez, Pierre   35, 70, 73, 96
Brahms, Johannes   3, **60**, 61, 85
Braille   43
Brass band notation   53, 95
Britten, Benjamin   30, 61, 70, **101**, 132
Brown, Earle   **55**, 146
Brumby, Colin   152 n.
Burney, Charles   31, 40
Bussotti, Sylvano   **144**
Button, Elliot   30
Byrd, William   **124**
Byzantine notation   7, **8**, 9, 37

Cage, John   69, 77, 124, 135, **136**, 139, 153
Carder, Malcolm   146
Cardew, Cornelius   37, 75, 124, 135, **136**, 140, 143, **145**, **146**, 148,
                                                                      152
Carter, Elliot   **72**, **96**
Cary, Tristram   115, **116**
Caxton, William   26

Cents (interval measurement)   109
Chinese notation   6, 7, 8, 9, 12, 38, 43
Chopin, Frederic   17, 49, 92
Conductors   42, 64, 93, 96
Connolly, Justin   73, 133
Conrad, Dr. R   15
Copland, Aaron   65, 66, 88, 91, 123
Copyright   10, 69
Cowell, Henry   52, 135

Daily Mirror   3
Dart, Thurston   14, 127
Delius, Frederick   91
Dennis, Brian   102, 103
Descriptive notation   16, 105, 115
Dobrowolski, A   113
Dowland, John   39, 43
Duo Art pianola   76

Electronic music notation   112-121
    Bibliographic uses of computer   118
    Computer music programs   119
    Descriptive notations   115
    Optical recognition devices   118, 121
    Wave-form notation   115
Elgar, Edward   84, 91
Ellis, Alexander John   109
Equiton   50, 137
Esperanto   13
Ethnomusicology   1, 4, 16, 105-110, 152
Eye movements   22

Feldman, Morton   56, 141
Ferguson, Howard   62
Figured bass   7, 137
Foss, Lukas   55, 56, 128, 129, 141
Fowles, Ernest   122

Gamut   100
Gerhard, Roberto   130
Gesture   42, 102
Gilbert, Anthony   91
God save the Queen   11, 102
Goehr, Walter   30
Gombrich, E.H.   14
Grame, T.C.   15

Handel, George Frideric   58
Harmonics   41, 53
Haubenstock-Ramati, Roman   81, 139
Helmholtz, Hermann   137 n.
Hindemith, Paul   48, 131
Holst, Gustav   67
Honegger, Arthur   18, 129
Hood, Mantle   78
Hornbostel, E. von   106 n.
Horror Fusae   29
Hukwe song   107, 108

Indeterminate notation   21, 33, 76, 137-140, 147
Irregular groups and rhythms   61, 62, 65, 67, 68, 88
Ives, Charles   51, 61, 126

Jacobs, Arthur   59
James, William   23, 150
Janáček, Leoš   24
Johnson, Jeremy   97

Kagel, Mauricio   43, 80, 126, 131, 133, 139, 140
Karkoshka, Erhard   151 n., 152
Keller, Hermann   85
Kitson, C.H.   130
Klavarscribe   49, 137
Krenek, Ernst   127, 129
Kupkovič, Ladislav   77

Lee, Vernon   122
Letter-notations   41
Light-signals   42
Lloyd, A.L.   74
Lumsdaine, David   70, 71
Lutoslawski, Wiltold   153

Macluhan, Marshall   36, 151
Mahler, Gustav   32 n., 85, 86
Mainardi, Enrico   99
Mainwaring, James   36
Martino, Donald   89, 90
Melograph   111
Messiaen, Olivier   61, 89, 94, 97
Milhaud, Darius   54, 55
Monteverdi, Claudio   31
Moran, Robert   143

Morley, Thomas   63, 148 n.
Morse code   13
Mozart, Wolfgang Amadeus   16, 64, 97, 118
Muffat, Georg   29, 37
Musicland bricks   103, 104

Neaman, Yfrah   62
Nettl, Bruno   79
Newman, Ernest   122

Ornament notation   4, 30, 31, 38 n.

Paradoxical notation   21, 69, 84, 140, 142
Parthenia   59
Penderecki, Krzysztof   52, 81, 135
Phonometer   74
Pope, Alexander   12
Pousseur, Henri   48, 138
Proportionate notation   27, 70, 71, 72, 73, 137
Purcell, Henry   37

Quarter tones   79

Ravel, Maurice   78
Read, Gardner   62, 103
Reynolds, Roger   37

Sachs, Curt   37
Schenker, Heinrich   87
Schoenberg, Arnold   64, 89, 92, 123, 127, 137, 138, 139
Schubert, Franz   34, 63, 98
Schumann, Robert   66, 124
Seashore, Carl   129
Seeger, Charles   109, 111
Self, George   102
Sessions, Roger   98
Sibelius, Jean   94
Simpson, Christopher   68
Smalley, Roger   146
Snap-pizzicato   79
Socrates   149 n.
Sound-signals as notation   42
Staccato   14, 82
Stockhausen, Karlheinz   50, 62, 69, 72, 73, 75, 76, 77, 89, 92, 113,
                          114, 117, 132, 134, 135, 138, 139, 140, 141
Stokowski, Leopold   74

Stone, Kurt   71, 152
Strauss, Johann   63
Strauss, Richard   28, 65
Stravinsky, Igor   34, 62, 64, 65, 67, 68, 83, 89, 91, 112, 127, 129, 132, 152

Takemitsu, Toru   146
Tchaikovsky, Piotr Ilyich   75, 76, 98
Thomas, Nancy   97
Thompson, D'Arcy Wentworth   36
Tippett, Michael   88
Transposition   41, 53
Trial (voice)   78

Universal Edition   29
Ussachevsky, Vladimir   10

Wagner, Richard   64, 68, 87
Walton, William   34, 74, 75
Weber, Carl Maria von   124
Webern, Anton von   85, 146
Wolff, Christian   140, 141, 142

Xenakis, Iannis   42, 147

Zinovieff, Peter   113, 120, 121